Margaret Atwood's Apocalypses

Margaret Atwood's Apocalypses

Edited by

Karma Waltonen

Cambridge
Scholars
Publishing

Margaret Atwood's Apocalypses

Edited by Karma Waltonen

This book first published 2015

Cambridge Scholars Publishing

Lady Stephenson Library, Newcastle upon Tyne, NE6 2PA, UK

British Library Cataloguing in Publication Data
A catalogue record for this book is available from the British Library

ISBN (10): 1-4438-6882-5
ISBN (13): 978-1-4438-6882-2

For the Margaret Atwood Society, my community of Atwoodians, which organised the MLA panel that inspired this book.

For the Margaret Atwood Book Group, which has met weekly at my house since 2005.

For Margaret Atwood, who writes about darkness so that we may see the light.

CONTENTS

INTRODUCTION

"[IT] WAS ZERO HOUR, YOU SAID BE BRAVE": TRACING ATWOOD'S APOCALYPSES[1]

Apocalypses and Beginnings

For much of my youth, I was put off by dystopic visions. I'm not sure if this was because I was so frightened of what my own future could become, if I was horrified by the dark glimpses into human nature that dystopias provide or because I'd been frightened by a childhood viewing of an HBO special on Nostradamus, featuring explorations of a coming apocalypse that were rather hysterical (in both senses of the word). I eschewed all of the texts that would later captivate me (like *Bladerunner*) and settled on comforting visions of the future (like the socialist near paradise that was *Star Trek*). Then, in high school, there was *The Handmaid's Tale*. One relative, who had not read the book, but who had heard some rumours about it, tried to deny me access, even though it was required reading. Luckily, I prevailed. It entranced me, both with its ideas and its language—which could be poetic and tragic and comic all at the same time. When Aunt Lydia tells the girls that they are rare and valued, like pearls, our narrator contemplates the metaphor: "I think about pearls. Pearls are congealed oyster spit" (145)—it was exactly the type of close reading that I was prone to do.

Perhaps the text drew me in because I identified with it. Atwood wrote parts of the novel in Alabama, very near where I was growing up (in "Florbama"—the part of Florida directly underneath Alabama). Her world seemed very real to me—I was deep in the Bible belt; our world history teacher was forbidden to acknowledge that there was any history before the ancient Egyptians, as that fact offended parents who believed the Earth was only 6000 years old; abstinence only education was standard; an

---

[1] Many ideas in this introduction were originally shared at an MLA panel, organised by the Margaret Atwood Society, in 2012.

abortion provider, David Gunn, was murdered in my town right around the time we encountered the handmaid's repressive society.

I was electrified. Not all students responded the same way, of course. I remember one girl complaining that she didn't like the book because it was disturbing. And I remember the teacher's response: "Good. It's supposed to disturb you."

A fuse was lit—I went on to read all of Atwood and to expand my love of science-fiction so that it might include the dystopic, the disturbing. My trajectory has coincided with a rise in apocalyptic works in popular culture, providing more evidence to the theory among scholars that Atwood has an eerily accurate foresight of our culture's trends. The theme of apocalypse did not start with *The Handmaid's Tale*, however.

The first two poems in *The Circle Game*, one of Atwood's earliest works, are both concerned with the idea of apocalypse. "This is a Photograph of Me" presents a landscape in which the narrator is in a liminal space—there but not there—presumably drowned but still conscious enough to narrate. "After the Flood We" features a speaker heading to higher ground, wondering if anyone else besides the visible and oblivious companion has survived a flood that has fish "swimming / down in the forest beneath us" (18). These tropes appear throughout Atwood's oeuvre —we have liminal narrators suffering through catalytic changes in *Bodily Harm*, *The Handmaid's Tale* and *The Penelopiad*. "The Flood" appears in another form in the *MaddAddam* trilogy. In other words, Atwood's interest in the apocalypse, interpreted as personal, national and global destruction, has roots in her earliest works. Is it Crake or Jimmy who might be conceived in "You did it" (*Power Politics*)—the one "who started the countdown / . . . on whom the demonic number / zero descended" (32); which man has begun the "zero hour" of the end of the world? Atwood, throughout her entire career, has been our Cassandra, describing "the howling that's going on outside, day and night, among the sand dunes and the ice chunks and the ruins and bones and so forth" (*The Tent* 144).

There are several definitions of apocalypse. One is extreme—an ELE—extinction level event. Others are end times, which can be defined more specifically—the end of a civilization, population, world, time, relationship or individual life. The older definition is of revelation—truth revealed in a time of darkness.

All of these definitions are inherent in Atwood's body of work. Most people, when they think of her apocalyptic work, focus on *The Handmaid's Tale* and the *MaddAddam* series. In *The Handmaid's Tale*, we have the threat of the end of a certain kind of civilization due to low birth rates, pollution, a government overthrow, a war, and then, at the very end, a discussion of a now-extinct civilization. *MaddAddam* gives us the end of the known world, first through scientific, cultural and environmental disasters, and then through Crake's waterless flood.

Earl G. Ingersoll claims that Atwood invites us to see *Oryx and Crake* as "book end" to *The Handmaid's Tale*, and thus we are to read the works together (162). Certainly, we can relate the other pieces she's written as well, focusing on her visions about what we do to the earth and to each other.

Let us first address general apocalypses of various kinds. As I've already mentioned, the first substantial poetry collection contained a death (perhaps by landscape) in "This is a Photograph of Me", with the second poem describing the actions of two survivors after a cataclysmic flood. In "Winter Sleepers" (*Circle*), the diluvian theme continues:

Outside, the land
is filled with drowning men (59)

The flood symbolises the narrator's father's stroke in "Wave" (*Morning in the Burned House*):

He was sitting in a chair at dinner
and a wave washed over him.
Suddenly, whole beaches
were simply gone.
1947. Lake Superior. Last year. (83)

Similarly, *The Labrador Fiasco* conflates the fading of the father with the failed Hubbard & Wallace expedition of the arctic. This is similar to watching "My Mother [dwindle]" (*The Door*): "It's like watching somebody drown" (16).

This reminds us of the personal apocalypse in every story—highlighted in "Happy Endings" (*Murder in the Dark*)—"John and Mary die. John and Mary die. John and Mary die" (40). (I will not highlight every death in all of Atwood's work, for the sake of time, but since she's writing about us—and we inevitably die—there are many).

Thus, apocalypse is everywhere. In "Spring Poem" (*You Are Happy*): "apocalypse [is] coiled in my tongue" (23). There are dreams in "Tree Baby" (*The Tent*): "Will they call it Catastrophe . . . Or will they call it Beginning" (151). The narrator "had become a visitant from outer space, a time-traveller come back from the future, bearing news of a great disaster" (*Bluebeard's Egg* 23) in "Significant Moments in the Life of My Mother".

Even the cat gets in on it when, in "Our Cat Enters Heaven" (*The Tent*), the cat is "raptured" (63).

Survival: As Plan and Theme

The other side of the Janus head known as disaster is survival, a theme so prevalent in Atwood's writing and Canadian literature as a whole that we have Atwood's foundational work about Canadian literature, *Survival*.

For stories of apocalypse to be told, someone must survive (at least temporarily)—long enough to be described or to narrate the end for an imagined future audience. This need for a narrator—for at least the hope of survival—has been with us since Mary Shelley's *The Last Man* (which gave us one of the great tropes of science fiction).

The first poem in *The Animals in that Country*, "Provisions", is about how explorers couldn't decide what to take and now they're "on the disastrous ice" with the wrong things (1).

In "The accident has occurred" (*Power Politics*), a question is raised:

> The accident has occurred,
> the ship has broken, the motor
> of the car has failed, we have been
> separated from the others,
> we are alone in the sand, the ocean,
> the frozen snow. . .
> Which of us will survive
> which of us will survive the other. (23)

An earlier poem in *The Circle Game* ("The explorers"), discusses what would happen after the skeletons of the explorers were found by others:

> (they won't be able
> to tell how long
> we were cast away, or why,
> or, from these
> gnawed bones,
> which was the survivor). (93)

Planning how to survive an unnamed possible disaster is the main theme in "When It Happens" in *Dancing Girls* (the first short story collection). Mrs Burridge is putting up her pickled green tomatoes. Then she's looking out the back door:

> She isn't sure what she is looking for but she has the odd idea she may see something burning, smoke coming up from the horizon, a column of it or perhaps more than one column, off to the south. (127)

She worries that her husband can't protect her or will be dead when it happens:

> Mrs. Burridge is not positive about what will happen next; that is, she knows what will happen but she is not positive about the order. She expects it will be the gas and oil: the oil delivery man will simply not turn up at his usual time, and one morning the corner filling station will be closed. . . they do not want people to panic . . . the phone goes dead . . . About now men begin to appear on the back road, the gravel road that goes past the gate, walking usually by themselves, sometimes in pairs . . . It is about this time too that she takes one of the guns . . . and hides it . . . With the electricity off they can no longer get the television . . . One morning she goes to the back door and looks out and there are columns of smoke, right where she's been expecting to see them, off to the south. (131-133)

Zero

Eula Biss, in her essay "The Pain Scale", notes:

> The description of hurricane force winds on the Beaufort scale is simply "devastation occurs".

> Bringing us, of course, back to zero. (42)

One of the major motifs that flows through many dystopian works is the number zero, symbolizing, among other things, the number of creatures we have alive after the process of extinction is complete. It is the number of annihilation.

In "The Line: Five Variations" (*The Door*), we have

> The monster not a burning coal,
> but ice-furred shadow. . . //
> in the midst of his blizzard,
> in the midst of his avalanches
> of *nihilo*,
> going about his business,
> wringing stars out of zero. (88)

"At first I was given centuries" (*Power Politics*) details many different bad endings over centuries between our couple in the collection:

And last time (I drove to the airport
still dressed in my factory
overalls, the wrench
I had forgotten sticking out of the back
pocket; there you were,
zippered and helmeted, it was zero
hour, you said Be
Brave . . . (28)

Of course, we can connect this poem from 1971 to the end of 2003's *Oryx and Crake*, as Jimmy considers his possibly suicidal and homicidal confrontation with the survivors on the beach:

From habit he lifts his watch; it shows him its blank face.
Zero hour, Snowman thinks. Time to go. (374)

When Bad News Is Old News

Through another motif (illustrated by a poem title), we are reminded that "It is dangerous to read newspapers" (*Animals in that Country*). The first story in *Moral Disorder* is "The Bad News".

Environmental disasters, a specific type of apocalypse, are also signalled by the dailies. We are told that "Chicken Little read too many newspapers" (*The Tent* 67). In this fable, he is not wrong at all, just inconvenient for everyone (like Al Gore). He is murdered with the excuse "He's against progress" (*The Tent* 71).

"The Age of Lead" mentions the Franklin Expedition. Then,

[the protagonist] began to notice news items of the kind she'd once skimmed over. Maple groves dying of acid rain, hormones in the beef, mercury in the fish, pesticides in the vegetables, poison sprayed on the fruit, God knows what in the drinking water. (*Wilderness Tips* 207)

In "Hack Wednesday", our narrator considers a fate for humanity that we have only begun to consider seriously in the last decade, though Atwood was obviously concerned much earlier (*Wilderness Tips*):

For a moment [Marcia] pictures what these squeaky-clean tiled tunnels would be like overgrown with moss or festooned with giant ferns; or underwater, when the greenhouse effect really gets going. She notices that she is no longer thinking in terms of *if*—only of *when*. She must watch this tendency to give up, she must get herself under control" (291-2).

Later, she notes, "It's all this talk of babies, at Christmas. It's all this hope. She gets distracted by it, and has trouble paying attention to the real news" (297).

Many environmental disasters are about the way we make the news. For examples, in "Eating the Birds" (*Tent*), "We're ankle-deep in blood, and all because we ate the birds, we ate them a long time ago, when we still had the power to say no" (129).

"Interview With a Tourist" (*Procedures*) gives us a foreign planet, with an inhabitant being interviewed by someone with a "camera and your spear":

> Once, when there was history
> some obliterating fact occurred,
> no solution was found
>
> Now this country is underwater;
> we can love only the drowned (23)

Ultimately, we are urged to follow the advice in "They are hostile nations" (*Power Politics*):

> In view of the fading animals
> the proliferation of sewers and fears
> the sea clogging, the air
> nearing extinction
>
> we should be kind, we should
> take warning, we should forgive each other. (37)

What Was At the Bottom of Pandora's Box

This idea of how we *might* respond is tied to an idea of hope—the very idea that we *can* respond provokes a sense of hope for ourselves and for a time of "we" "after the flood".

Although our author and her narrators "tell dark stories / before and after they come true" (*Door* 98), those stories are told to prevent the disasters foretold.

"Hopeless" (*Murder in the Dark*) notes,

> Hope needs the future tense, which only makes you greedy and a hoarder: the future is what you save up for but like thunder it's only an echo, a reverse dream. . . . This is as good as it gets, nothing can be better so there's nothing to hope for, but I do it anyway. (57)

Two works in *The Tent* explicitly discuss the need for hope. "Three Novels I Won't Write Soon" includes a treatment for *Worm Zero* in which all of the worms in the world die, leading to famine. The narrator says she would probably end "on a note of plangent hope" because she prefers that type of ending (88).[2]

The title story, "The Tent", vividly describes the act and purpose of writing as a struggle for hope:

> Some of the writing has to describe the howling that's going on outside, night and day, among the sand dunes and the ice chunks and the ruins and bones and so forth. (144)

However, there are no illusions that writers will be listened to any more than Cassandra:

> they resent being cooped up in such a cramped space with you and your obsession with calligraphy. . . . It's an illusion, the belief that your doodling is a kind of armour, a kind of charm, because no one knows better than you do how fragile your tent really is. (145-146)

Atwood's dystopic novels garner the most attention—from critics and fans—and they allow us to see most clearly her ability to foresee social, environmental and scientific trends. However, as this brief overview shows, we should recognise that her concern for the earth and its species—including the one that reads and writes—has been evident in her writing from the very beginning.

Atwood's career-long effort to bear witness is through her writing. Recently, she published a piece of short fiction ("Time Capsule Found on the Dead Planet") in *I'm With the Bears: Short Stories from a Damaged Planet*:

> In the fourth age we created deserts. Our deserts were of several kinds, but they had one thing in common: nothing grew there. Some were made of cement, some were made of various poisons, some of baked earth. We made these deserts from the desire for more money and from despair at the lack of it. War, plagues and famines visited us, but we did not stop in our industrious creation of deserts. At last all wells were poisoned, all rivers ran with filth, all seas were dead; there was no land left to grow food.
>
> Some of our wise men turned to the contemplation of deserts. . . . The number zero was holy. (192-193)

---

[2] Each of the three stories is similar. This short piece is followed by "Take Charge", outlining several disastrous scenarios.

With just a few short paragraphs, Atwood gives us an apocalypse, how the social mores of the survivors evolve and a pun.

And in that, there is hope.

Across these man-made, man-helped, and man-indifferent apocalypses —in burned houses, blizzards and floods—we find the themes of survival and hope, even when survival seems unlikely. We read these stories as the characters read the newspapers—as a revelation of the truth. This focus on truth through observation, however, challenges us to do more than be a passive observer. We should not be Offred, waiting until it's too late to fight or run. We should not be Jimmy, claiming innocence through passivity.

We must not simply observe. We must bear witness. We must act.

Our Text

Lauren Rule Maxwell's piece, "'[A]pocalypse coiled in my tongue': Apocalyptic Vision in Margaret Atwood's Poetry", is an excellent overview of our theme in what is arguably Atwood's first genre—in her exemplary close reading of several poems, she reminds us that while apocalypse may be coiled on the tongue, the Mobius strip of the possible end also contains a beginning.

Meredith Minister's essay, "The Languages are Being Silenced: Ambivalent Apocalyptic Vision in Margaret Atwood's Poems", also looks at poetry, digging deeply into the imagery of three poems in particular— "The Signer", "Marsh Languages" and "Half-Hanged Mary" (all from *Morning in the Burned House*)—to explore the relationship of language to agency, embodiment and apocalypse.

In our next essay, Patricia A. Stapleton's "Suicide as Apocalypse in *The Handmaid's Tale*", the personal apocalypse and the societal level apocalypse tragically come together. Stapleton convincingly argues that Offred's story of the Nazi mistress and other textual events foreshadow how Offred's own story will end—by the taking of her own life.

Anna Lindhé's "Restoring the Divine within: The Inner Apocalypse in Margaret Atwood's *The Year of the Flood*" takes us to Atwood's apocalypse opus, the *MaddAddam* series. The essay explores how societal apocalypse opens the doors to personal redemption, concluding,

> to restore harmony with the natural world as well as healthy social relations, humanity, Atwood suggests, needs to restore the divine within, or those ethical aspects of human life, which have somehow been lost: the caring other-oriented emotions of gratitude, charity, forgiveness and love.

Miles Weafer's "Writing from the Margin" also investigates *The Year of the Flood*, by combining Atwood's views on victim positions from her seminal study of Canadian Literature, *Survival*, and Harold Innis's conception of marginality. His analysis of *The Year of the Flood* indicates that "the more marginalised the victim, the better opportunity they have of achieving creative non-victimhood".

Finally, Anna Bedford's piece on the *MaddAddam* series, "Survival in the Post-Apocalypse", argues that Atwood's contribution to apocalypse literature is her modern ecofeminism, which holds that capitalism (one of the main contributors to the apocalypse in the series) exploits the most marginalised and powerless, including the poor, women and nature itself.

Works Cited

Atwood, Margaret. *The Animals in that Country*. London: Oxford University Press, 1975. Print.

—. *Bluebeard's Egg and Other Stories*. New York: Fawcett Crest, 1983. Print.

—. *The Circle Game*. Toronto: Anansi, 1966. Print.

—. *Dancing Girls and Other Stories*. New York: Bantam Books, 1977. Print.

—. *The Door*. Boston: Houghton Mifflin Company, 2007. Print.

—. *The Handmaid's Tale*. New York: Fawcett Crest, 1985. Print.

—. *The Labrador Fiasco*. London: Bloomsbury, 1996. Print.

—. *Moral Disorder and Other Stories*. New York: Nan A. Talese, 2006. Print.

—. *Morning in the Burned House*. Boston: Houghton Mifflin Company, 1995. Print.

—. *Murder in the Dark*. Toronto: Coach House Press, 1983. Print.

—. *Oryx and Crake*. New York: Anchor House, 2003. Print.

—. *Power Politics*. Toronto: Anansi, 1971. Print.

—. *Procedures for Underground*. Toronto: Oxford University Press, 1970. Print.

—. *The Tent*. New York: Nan A. Talese, 2006. Print.

—. "Time Capsule Found on the Dead Planet." *I'm With the Bears*. Ed. Mark Martin. New York: Verso, 2011. 191-193. Print.

—. *You Are Happy*. New York: Harper & Row, 1974. Print.

Biss, Eula. "The Pain Scale." *Touchstone Anthology of Contemporary Creative Nonfiction*. Eds. Lex Williford and Michael Martone. New York: Touchstone, 2007. 28-42. Print.

Ingersoll, Earl G. "Survival in Margaret Atwood's Novel *Oryx and Crake*". *Extrapolation* 45.2 (2004): 162-175. Print.

CHAPTER ONE

"[A]POCALYPSE COILED IN MY TONGUE": APOCALYPTIC VISION IN MARGARET ATWOOD'S POETRY[1]

LAUREN RULE MAXWELL

With the recent publication of *MaddAddam*, much has been written about Margaret Atwood's speculative fiction and its apocalyptic warnings. Scholars have revisited novels such as *Oryx and Crake*, *The Year of the Flood* and *The Handmaid's Tale* to discuss their environmental and human disasters and the lessons that these dystopian visions offer us. This focus on Atwood's speculative fiction, though fruitful, has largely overlooked the apocalyptic vision in Atwood's poetry. In this chapter, I will consider a sampling of poems from several of Atwood's collections—including *The Animals in That Country* (1969), *Power Politics* (1971), *You Are Happy* (1974), *Two-Headed Poems* (1978), *True Stories* (1981), *Interlunar* (1984) and *The Door* (2007)—to characterise what I call a sustained apocalyptic vision in Atwood's body of poetry. Many of Atwood's poems reference possible apocalypse; in them we find different apocalyptic visions that involve interpersonal, environmental and metaphysical relationships. These poems reveal in different contexts the potential of and for great disaster, not only underscoring a threat of utter destruction, but also representing the possibility for regeneration, rebirth and change that might be possible if the destruction does not go too far. In the poems that invoke apocalypse, Atwood suggests that there is a time for dying and a time for sowing, reflecting nature's own seasons. But what I find most interesting about this potential for disaster is the poet's ability—or lack thereof—to orchestrate it. This treatment of the word "apocalypse" asks us to consider

---

[1] A version of this paper was given at the MLA conference in 2012, at a panel organised by the Margaret Atwood Society.

the relationships of the poet and of language more generally to our conception of apocalypse itself.

One poem that raises these questions is "Spring Poem", from the 1974 collection *You Are Happy*. "Spring Poem" uses a seasonal trope to convey the potential for rebirth associated with disaster, but it also focuses very explicitly on the relationship of language to apocalypse that I'll focus on in this chapter. In the first few lines of the poem, the speaker discusses the decision to begin "burning / last year's weeds" and tells us that "the earth / ferments like rising bread / or refuse" (1-3). The poem's opening, by describing the fermentation as either "rising bread" or "refuse", suggests that destruction caused by the burning can bring about a transformation that creates, alternatively, sustenance or waste. The entire first stanza, 20 lines in total, draws attention to ways that language itself both signals and brings about transition and transformation through its unconventional use of punctuation. Until line 17—where we see the end of the question "can I be this / ruthless?"—there is no end punctuation (16-17). The absence of terminal punctuation is pronounced because commas and virgules appear within the lines where one might expect periods. Instead of ending the thought "It is spring", the speaker turns it, signalling shifts with the downward marks of the comma and the slash, creating with the words on the page what resembles a corkscrew. The images in this spiralling design pan around the fermented earth, showing us the changes to the landscape that the decision to burn has set into motion.

We first see what is happening to the atmosphere, the air above ground: "the smoke / flares from the road" (4-5). Then the frame moves downward to the "clumped stalks" that "glow like sluggish phoenixes" (5, 6). The images that follow "sidewind[]", leading us closer and closer to ground level:

> only my fault / the birdsongs burst from
> the feathered pods of their bodies, dandelions
> whirl their blades upwards, from beneath
> this decaying board a snake,
> sidewinds, the chained hide
> smelling of reptile sex / the hens
> roll in the dust, squinting with bliss, frogbodies
> bloat like bladders, contract, string
> the pond with living jelly
>
> eyes, can I be this
> ruthless? I plunge
> my hands and arms into the dirt,
> swim among stones and cutworms,
> come up rank as a fox. (7-20)

Like the snake, the poem moves, swaying from side to side. And, like the snake, the poem's spine reveals a chain: both lines and images are links interconnected. The poem's speaker depicts the organisms that inhabit this ecosystem and thus are commonly affected by the burning—those damaged or displaced by the decision, which, the speaker asserts, is not actually "only my fault". In the preceding line, she asserts that "it wasn't", emphasising that claim by separating it from the surrounding images with virgules— "/ it wasn't" (6) and "only my fault /" (7). The line break after "wasn't" creates some ambiguity about whose responsibility this chain of events is, shedding some doubt on the speaker's initial statement that this is "my decision". It does not seem, however, that the burning has been wholly destructive; the stalks are likened to "phoenixes", and we see reproductive images, such as "reptile sex", that are suggestive of life to come. As the speaker contemplates whether or not she is "ruthless", she goes below the surface, submerging her hands and arms in the dirt. Earlier in the poem, the speaker actually prefigures this breaking ground with the words "my fault", which, in addition to representing her responsibility, can suggest her own fracturing of the earth's surface.

With this act of going underground, the speaker, as with other women in Atwood's poetry, delves into the subterranean space of her own consciousness. Signalling a reflective pause, the first period in "Spring Poem" appears after the first word in the second stanza, "restless". Having "restless" precede the period further emphasises the momentum of the first stanza, movement that resumes after the appearance of those she has hurt:

> restless. Nights, while seedlings
> dig near my head
> I dream of reconciliations
> with those I have hurt
> unbearably, we move still (21-25)

Here, the seedlings, not the speaker, are doing the digging, and her subconscious tries to reconcile the fact that she has hurt. The word "unbearably" in line 25 might refer to those she has hurt, claiming agency as the one who has hurt them (or hurt herself), or those who "move still". Regardless, there is a sense that aspects of this cycle of destruction and reconstruction are unbearable, perhaps unsustainable. During the day she goes for "vicious walks past the charred / roadbed over the bashed stubble / admiring the view" (29-31). It is not clear if she is admiring what remains, "those I have not hurt" or the "bashed stubble" from which will presumably eventually emerge new growth (32, 30).

Although the speaker is "avoiding / those I have not hurt", she has the
power, latent as it might be, of destruction more final and complete—of
apocalypse (31-32). The last stanza evokes it explicitly:

> yet, apocalypse coiled in my tongue,
> it is spring, I am searching
> for the word:
> > finished
> > finished
>
> so I can begin over
> again, some year
> I will take this word too far. (33-40)

In these closing lines of "Spring Poem", the speaker repeats the opening
clause of the poem: "It is spring", but in this context the line has a
different meaning. At the beginning of the poem we assume that the word
"spring" represents the season, the time of year, but at the end it becomes
clear to us that the speaker is now figuring apocalypse itself as a spring
coiled in her tongue. The placement of the words in this last stanza, as
those in the first, resembles the shape of a spring with its spiralled
corkscrew, suggesting that the words on the page possess—like a
compressed spring—some latent power, some potential momentum that
will be unleashed once they are unfurled. The anaphora in the poem, seen
in lines like "it is spring" and "finished", helps assemble the repeating turns
in the helix. The turning is reinforced by the images in the poem, which run
together, emphasised by the places where they are separated within a line by
a slash. This stream of images, comprising the spring's connected curves,
builds tension until we reach the catalytic word—apocalypse.

    That the poem's form mirrors its content is important because it draws
attention to the power of language itself, which becomes the final focus of
the poem. As the speaker searches for a word to describe the "apocalypse
coiled in [her] tongue", she finally settles on "finished", a word that she
repeats, complicating its meaning. If "finished" represented a true finality,
there would be no need for it to be repeated. This word, she tells us,
counterintuitively allows her to "begin over / again". In the very same line,
however, she adds—connecting these ideas with only a comma—that
"some year / I will take this word too far". Thus the apocalypse is
associated with an incomplete finish that could allow for a new beginning
or—if she takes the word too far—could be the final end. It is as though
the possibility for the true finish represented by the word "apocalypse"
helps bring about these nonpermanent finishes that eventually give way to
new life. The writer is like the persona, who burned the last year's weeds

and cleared a path, in that she completes one work and moves on to the next. The landscape is marked by this change, as seen in the "charred / roadbed", but nevertheless there are those who survive and move on—some with "living jelly / eyes", who have seen but might not be able to bear witness to the destruction that changed their worlds. That is the job of the artist, who can warn of the hurt caused by our destructive behaviours by the mere mention of the word "apocalypse".

With lines like "I dream of reconciliations / with those I have hurt / unbearably", "Spring Poem" reflects upon failed interpersonal relationships. But the poem's ending focuses more specifically on words: with its coiled apocalypse, it suggests that words themselves have the power to make things happen. Although we don't see the words themselves hurting or terrorising, we know they have that power. Knowing that "apocalypse [is] coiled" in the speaker's "tongue", we are left to imagine what exactly it would mean for her to "take this word too far", but we are nonetheless reminded why words matter. As Atwood emphasises in her much-anthologised poem "Spelling" (*True Stories* 1981), "A word after a word / after a word is power" (24-25). In "Spelling", the speaker considers her daughter's playing with plastic letters "learning how to spell, / spelling, / how to make spells", a theme Atwood explores in another work from her collection *You Are Happy* (1974), the cycle of the "Circe/Mud Poems". From the very beginning of this series, we see words' importance in the creation of spells and even entire worlds.

In the first cycle of the "Circe/Mud Poems", Circe says that Odysseus "move[s] within the range of my words" (*Selected Poems* 201). She goes on to describe the men she has changed to beasts, repeating—with an assertion that echoes that of the speaker of "Spring Poem"—"It is not my fault", "it was not my fault", but she nonetheless suggests that the change was brought about by her control of language:

It was not my fault, these animals
who once were lovers

it was not my fault, the snouts
and hooves, the tongues
thickening and rough, the mouths grown over
with teeth and fur

I did not add the shaggy
rugs, the tusked masks,
they happened

I did not say anything, I sat

and watched, they happened
because I did not say anything.

It was not my fault, these animals
who could no longer touch me
through the rinds of their hardening skins,
these animals dying
of thirst because they could not speak

these drying skeletons
that have crashed and litter the ground
under the cliffs, these
wrecked words. (*Selected Poems* 203)

Words shape everything in Circe's world, including the landscape itself, whose cliffs she calls "wrecked words". It is clear that her words control the fate of her former lovers—creating for them an apocalypse of life as they knew it—regardless of whether it is because she casts a spell on them or, in her words, "because [she] did not say anything". The men, transformed, are dying, Circe tells us, precisely because they cannot speak. But Circe empowers her chosen one, Odysseus, by naming for him the features of her island, observing that he "claim[s] / without noticing it"— that he "know[s] how to take" (*Selected Poems* 209). By "pronouncing these names" for Odysseus, she gives him knowledge, gives him power. But Odysseus responds by physically overpowering her body: in parentheses we read, "Let go, this is extortion, / you force my body to confess / too fast and / incompletely" (*Selected Poems* 210). Her words, her body's words, have become "tongueless and broken" (*Selected Poems* 210). In "Spring Poem", we see that the power of the word comes from the latent energy, the potential momentum building behind it. Instead of the coiled apocalypse there, the curved spirals of Circe's spells have been broken, at least for the moment. And because she is "tongueless", her words cannot spring forth: although words unspoken might have potential, those spoken (or written) can move others and cause the type of revolutionary change we see in the transformation of the men to beasts. Circe says that these transformations happened "because [she] did not say anything", but here we see the real difference between choosing not to speak and being unable to. As Circe and Odysseus jockey for power, its balance has apparently shifted; Odysseus writing his "travel book" worries Circe, who wants to be able to tell her side of the story (*Selected Poems* 217).

Circe later reminds us, however, "it is not finished, that saga": "The fresh monsters are already breeding in my head" (*Selected Poems* 217).

While she flippantly says, "So much for art. So much for prophesy", she later clarifies that "[t]o know the future / there must be a death" and commands, "[h]and me the axe" (*Selected Poems* 217, 219). The future, she knows, "is a mess" (*Selected Poems* 217). But what in fact undoes Circe's spell and wrecks her world is language, not an axe and not Odysseus. "It's the story that counts," she tells us:

> In the story the boat disappears one day over the horizon, just disappears, and it doesn't say what happens then. On the island that is. It's the animals I am afraid of, they weren't part of the bargain, in fact you don't mention them, they may transform themselves back into men. Am I really immortal, does the sun care, when you leave will you give me back the words? (*Selected Poems* 221)

These questions, directed presumably at Odysseus, reveal that, ultimately, the things that constitute Circe's world and her possible immortality are words. Without them, she, the animals, the entire island disappear.

The reordering of the world through language appears also in Atwood's poem "Progressive Insanities of a Pioneer" from the 1968 collection *The Animals in That Country*. In this poem, the pioneer proclaims himself from the first stanza of the poem the "centre" of the earth (3). But even from the very beginning, Atwood emphasises the constructedness of our worlds, the degree to which we rely on representation of the things themselves, by describing him as "a point / on a sheet of green paper / proclaiming himself the centre" (1-3). The paper, something that is made of vegetative material, might be a map, might be the page on which the poet writes her words or might be a metaphor. In "Murder and Mayhem: Margaret Atwood Deconstructs", Lorna Irvine examines Atwood's use of metaphor in works such as *Murder in the Dark,* focusing specifically on the following passage from "Spelling":

> At the point where language falls away
> from the hot bones, at the point
> where the rock breaks open and darkness
> flows out of it like blood, at
> the melting point of granite
> when the bones know
> they are hollow & the word
> splits & doubles & speaks
> the truth & the body itself becomes a mouth.
>
> This is a metaphor. (275)

As Irvine asserts, Atwood "imagines an altered metaphor" that brings about "the visions and the thinking necessary to sustain, console and alter human existence—a new relationship to the universe" (275). Atwood's use of metaphor, such as her use of the word "paper" in "Progressive Insanities of a Pioneer", can cause us to see the world in a different way, to reconsider our traditional relationships in it. Like the word "apocalypse" in "Spring Poem", the right word in a poem has the power to transform our vision and our thinking. Irvine explains:

> Only by the power of the right word, the generative word, will murder in the dark be changed, be transformed to birth in the light.

"Metaphor is dangerous", she says, "but it can also perhaps save" (275). From the very beginning of "Progressive Insanities of a Pioneer", Atwood invokes the metaphors of the point and of the paper to highlight the disconnected relationship we have with the natural world and the ways our attempts to contain, control and possess become evident when examining the language we use out of context: papers might confer ownership of the land to the pioneer, but when he himself becomes merely a point on a green sheet of paper, we see more clearly how we have abstracted nature to the point that we do not really see it at all. In doing so, Atwood highlights "the tension / between subject and object" that eventually does the pioneer in (79-80).

When the pioneer stands in the middle of the green sheet, there are "no walls, no borders / anywhere; the sky no height / above him, totally un- / enclosed" (4-7). "Let me out!" he exclaims, feeling trapped in the open, free expanse (9). The pioneer needs to make his mark on the place—he is compelled to contain, organise, control—so he "dug the soil in rows, / imposed himself with shovels. / [and] asserted / into the furrows, I / am not random" (10-14). The ground, however, "replied with aphorisms: // a tree-sprout, a nameless / weed, words / he couldn't understand" (17-19). By giving the ground a voice, Atwood both draws our attention to its existence, complete with life of its own, and demonstrates for us that it has its own ways of communicating that we do not understand. The disjunction in language becomes even more pronounced as the pioneer's madness grows. Being "disgusted / with the swamp's clamourings and the outbursts / of rocks", he says, "This is not order / but the absence / of order" (34-36, 37-39). When the "unanswering forest" implies that "[i]t was / an ordered absence", we see clearly the importance of word order itself (40, 42-43). By inverting the order of the words "absence" and "order", the entire perspective of the poem changes, reversing who is in control and what the signs in the landscape mean. The pioneer is clearly not in control here; something else, either the "unanswering forest" or his own madness is. There is also the implied threat—in the phrase "ordered absence"—of apocalypse, the forced end of human society as we know it, an end that would allow the natural order to begin again. In fact, the pioneer, "[o]n his beaches, his clearings, / by the surf of under- / growth breaking / at his feet" foresees "disintegration" (71-74, 75). This disintegration is brought on, at least in part, by language: "Things / refused to name themselves; refused / to let him name them" (66-68). One might argue that this apocalyptic scenario given life through words reflects only the pioneer's declining mental condition, but, then again, it might conversely reflect that he—or at least the poet presenting what is going on inside his head—is, in fact, seeing the world, or what the world might become, more clearly.

It is the work of the poet, Atwood explains in "Notes Towards a Poem That Can Never Be Written" (*True Stories* 1981), to provide this premonitory vision: when one sees "[t]he facts of this world...clearly", she asserts, "[w]itness is what you must bear" (42, 57). But as we see in the poem "Foretelling the Future" from *Two-Headed Poems* (1978), things appear differently depending on the various places from which they are seen. The poem reads: "you are like the moon / seen from the earth, oval and gentle / and filled with light", but "[t]he moon seen from the moon / is a different thing" (17-19, 20-21). As Atwood shows us in the poem "The Words Continue Their Journey" (*Interlunar* 1984), poets have a unique perspective that is both driven by and constituted with words. The poem begins with a question: "Do poets really suffer more / than other people?" (1-2). Suggesting that poets really do suffer more, the speaker goes on to tell us that the poets' occupying a distinct position makes them "members of some doomed caravan" (27). It is a collective condition in which they travel, "a pilgrimage that took a wrong turn / somewhere far back and ended / here, in the full glare" (34-36). The sun creates glare and shadows as the language does itself, the poets evoking their own "aureole of *stone*, of *tree*" (40). Ultimately the speaker concludes that, despite their words, the poets will have the same fate as everyone else:

we're no more doomed really than anyone, as we go / together, through this moon terrain / where everything is dry and perishing and so / vivid, into the dunes, vanishing out of sight. (41-44)

That is what the apocalypse that the poets warn of entails—vanishing: "vanishing out of the sight of each other, / vanishing even out of our own sight" (45-46).

In "The Poets Hang On", from the 2007 collection *The Door*, Atwood actually pokes fun at poets for professing to have this premonitory vision, for professing to know something the rest of the world doesn't. The poem begins:

> The poets hang on.
> It's hard to get rid of them,
> though lord knows it's been tried.
> We pass them on the road
> standing there with their begging bowls,
> an ancient custom.
> Nothing in those now
> but dried flies and bad pennies.
> They stare straight ahead.
> Are they dead, or what?
> Yet they have an irritating look
> of those that know more than we do. (1-12)

The poem ends with these lines:

> They know something, though.
> They do know something.
> Something they're whispering,
> something we can't quite hear.
> Is it about sex?
> Is it about dust?
> Is it about fear? (58-64)

This delightful poem satirises poets' pretensions of knowing better, but at the same time it suggests that there is something to the poet's premonitions, something that I associate with Atwood's larger apocalyptic vision. Is it about sex, dust or fear? Perhaps. The not-knowing makes Atwood's premonitory warnings even more captivating. But it is certain that the apocalyptic vision in Atwood's poetry consciously acknowledges the power of language itself to make us fear what we are capable of.

While the poet can control language and the power that comes with it, poems such as "Bluejays" (*True Stories* 1981) and "Disturbed Earth" (*The Door* 2007) show that there is much outside of the control of language and of order more generally. For example, in "Disturbed Earth", despite the gardener's attempt to create pristine perennial beds, a natural disorder "thwarts [her] will" (14). The speaker of "Bluejays" similarly predicts that next summer, after the bluejays eat her sunflowers, "something forgotten will bloom there" (26).

These poems show that although we make our mark on it, we ultimately don't control the earth. Likewise, we don't know what the end will be or when it will come. In "They Are Hostile Nations" (*Power Politics* 1971), we are warned that the end is possibly upon us. The poem begins:

In the view of the fading animals
the proliferation of sewers and fears
the sea clogging, the air
nearing extinction

we should be kind, we should
take warning, we should forgive each other

Instead we are opposite, we
touch as though attacking,

the gifts we bring
even in good faith maybe
warp in our hands to implements, to maneuvers[.] (1-12)

Facing the end, the great vanishing where we lose sight of others and ourselves, we do exactly the opposite of what we should: we seek to hurt rather than to mend. The poem's end warns us:

It is cold and getting colder
We need each others'
breathing, warmth, surviving
is the only war
we can afford, stay

walking with me, there is almost
time / if we can only
make it as far as

the (possibly) last summer[.] (25-33)

The last line of the poem charts an endpoint—"the (possibly) last summer". In this line, the word "possibly" is both subordinated and highlighted by appearing in parentheses. It is possibility itself that is ultimately at the heart of Atwood's apocalyptic vision: the possibility of the end and the possibility of living as if each day could be our last.

Works Cited

Atwood, Margaret. *The Animals in That Country*. Boston: Atlantic Little-
    Brown, 1968. Print.
—. *The Door*. Boston: Houghton Mifflin Company, 2007. Print.
—. *Interlunar*. Toronto: Oxford UP, 1974. Print.
—. *Power Politics*. Toronto: Anansi, 1971. Print.
—. *Selected Poems, 1965-1975*. Boston: Houghton Mifflin Company,
    1976. Print.
—. *True Stories*. New York: Simon and Schuster, 1981. Print.
—. *Two-Headed Poems*. New York: Simon and Schuster, 1978. Print.
—. *You Are Happy*. New York: Harper & Row, 1974. Print.
Irvine, Lorna. "Murder and Mayhem: Margaret Atwood Deconstructs".
    Contemporary Literature 24.2 (1988): 265-76.

CHAPTER TWO

THE LANGUAGES ARE BEING SILENCED: AMBIVALENT APOCALYPTIC VISION IN MARGARET ATWOOD'S POEMS

MEREDITH MINISTER

Margaret Atwood has been called an apocalyptic optimist (Thill), an outlook she says is necessary for writing the speculative ustopias that made her a literary star (Atwood "The Road"). While known primarily for her fiction, Atwood is also the author of numerous volumes of poetry that share a sense of the apocalyptic developed in her fiction. Although Atwood paints bleak pictures in which the human will to power ends in the destruction of life, her poetry undermines the historical futurity contained in her narrative prose and, thereby, offers a possible arrest to the impending apocalypse. In this chapter, I explore the theme of language and its role in the making and unmaking of the world in three of Atwood's poems from *Morning in the Burned House*: "The Signer", "Marsh Languages" and "Half-Hanged Mary". Through this exploration, I contend that Atwood describes a relationship between speech, bodies and life, which, if severed, will result in a death-dealing apocalypse. Understanding this integration of language, bodies and life, on the other hand, may have the power to prevent the impending apocalypse.

Disability in "The Signer"

"The Signer" draws on a scene in which an individual translating oral speech into sign language stands behind a speaker, presumably translating the speaker's speech for a deaf audience,

In city after city / in an area of darkness behind my head / stands a woman dressed in black, / even the stockings: my unknown twin.

Evoking the twin, the poem suggests a similarity between the speaker and the signer but also appears to avoid dissolving the crucial difference between the two. As the poem associates the speaker with language and the signer with bodies, "The Signer" offers a hopeful gesture toward the unification of language and bodies. The unification, however, threatens to dissolve the difference made present in the body of the signer and reify the ideology of ability. Atwood's "The Signer", thus works by drawing on and challenging cultural narratives that play ability and disability against one another. As the poem draws on and challenges disability tropes by materialising both the speaker and the signer, it reveals integral connections between ability and disability, language and bodies.

The poem shifts between maintaining the distinction between the speaker and the signer and collapsing the distinction between the speaker and the signer throughout the poem. In particular, the poem differentiates the signer from the speaker by playing the language of the speaker against the body of the signer:

> In her hands, deft as a knitter's / but quicker, my words turn solid, / become a gesture, a skein, / a semaphore of the body / for those who listen with their eyes . . . what puns of the thumb, tough / similes of the fingers, / how I translate into bone.

By associating the signer with a knitter's hands, a solid gesture, a skein, a body, a thumb, fingers, bones and the speaker with words, puns and similes, the poem suggests that language exists apart from bodies and must be translated into those bodies in order to be accessible to those who cannot escape from bodies. In this distinction, the signer operates bodily while the speaker might be said to speak a (presumably disembodied) language.

The poem introduces a further complexity into the description of the signer by attributing the signer with the mixed metaphors of absence and left-handedness, a mixture that reflects the cultural perception of disabled bodies that are both inconsequential and evil matter in need of perfecting. As Tobin Siebers describes,

> On the one hand, bodies do not seem to matter to who we are . . . On the other hand, modern culture feels the urgent need to perfect the body . . . We hardly ever consider how incongruous is this understanding of the body—that the body seems both inconsequential and perfectible. (7)

As left-handed, the body of the signer is associated with degradation and is, thus, in need of perfecting. As absent, the body of the signer is associated with something that literally does not matter. While poets may use mixed metaphors to develop a complex understanding of something assumed to be simple, the poem's mixed metaphors seem, at times, to play on the trope of the disabled body rather than subvert it.

In its attempt to distinguish between the speaker and the signer, the poem presses dangerously close to the ideology of ability. As Siebers describes the characteristics of the ideology of ability, "If one is able-bodied, one is not really aware of the body. One feels the body only when something goes wrong with it" (10). If disability is a phenomenon that is assumed to press someone into the body while an able-bodied person might presume to be disembodied, then the poem's association of the signer with the body and the speaker with language may be read as perpetuating an ideology of ability.

Although "The Signer" gestures toward disability tropes, it also undermines those tropes, first, by exploring language as bodily and, second, by unravelling the threads of translation that would locate the creative speaker in a superior relationship to the signer, who does not generate but translates. In exploring language as bodily, the poem suggests that the signer stands outside of the ideology of language, a position privileged (by its very lack of social privilege) to critique the ideology of language as immaterial. As Siebers describes, "Ideology creates, by virtue of its exclusionary nature, social locations outside of itself and therefore capable of making epistemological claims about it" (8). Because the signer is located between ability and disability, she occupies a privileged space that can critique the ideology of the disembodied immateriality of language. Although the signer herself must be able to hear the speaker, her status as a liminal figure who stands on the threshold of hearing and deafness in order to facilitate communication between worlds presses her into the body. In this interpretation, the signer takes on disability tropes by her proximity to disabled bodies. In her affiliation with deaf bodies, the signer exists on the spectrum of disability, an existence that identifies the limitations of the ability/disability binary. As Sharon Betcher describes,

> Becoming disabled *potentially* offers a line of flight for becoming revolutionary insofar as we take up our divergence from the norm not as a resistance, but as a creative edge, as a location for inventing new forms of subjectivity, rather than returning to the realm of ego and identity . . . The event of disability happens whenever any dares pass through the dizzying whirl of abjection psychically laid between disabled persons and the rest of the human community (174-5).

Insofar as the signer is afforded an opportunity to pass through the whirl of objection, the signer might be said to become disabled. The signer, therefore, reveals the spectrum of disability by operating in the liminal space between deaf persons and those who hear.

Moreover, the poem undermines disability tropes by unravelling the threads of translation that would suggest that the signer offers an accessible, bodily version of the speaker's presumably immaterial language. In particular, the poem equalises the speaker and the signer without equating them, "It is not a translation / you built here, mute sister". With this line, the poem denies the suggestion that the signer translates the speaker and the claim that the signer materialises the speaker. The poem's refusal to identify the work of the signer as translation realises the work of the signer apart from the language of the speaker and, thus, suggests that the work of the signer is not accessible to the speaker just as the speaker is not accessible to the signer. The signer, therefore, does not embody a complicated language to make it accessible, an embodiment that would assume that the speaker exists in the abstract, universal realm of language, while the signer translates into the concrete particular realm of the (disabled) body. The speaker and the signer, rather, inhabit two different realms. Such a difference highlights the complicated agency of disabled bodies, bodies that ablest frameworks attempt to fix as passive recipients.

This difference between the speaker and the signer collapses at two points in the poem. First, the distinction collapses when the poem draws on the metaphor of listening to describe how deaf people might watch the signer, "for those who listen with their eyes". As listening literally describes how the speaker's audience would process language audibly, the poem's use of listening as a metaphor for deaf communication threatens the distinction between speaker and signer she upholds at other places in the poem. The distinction between speaker and signer also collapses at the end of the poem as it imagines the future: "together we are practicing / for the place where all the languages / will be finalized and / one; and the hands also". Through these images, the poem suggests that this current difference between language and bodies will be resolved in the future, as the conclusion imagines a place where all languages and hands will be one when language is located in its bodily home.

While this conclusion contains a hopeful gesture toward universal communication, it achieves this communication by collapsing the difference the poem has maintained between the signer and the speaker at other points in the poem. In this concluding utopic gesture toward a unification of language and bodies, the potential hope of the poem's apocalyptic gesture turns as the signer and the speaker lose their distinctiveness and are threatened by a homogenising apocalypse. Here, ablest narratives threaten to silence disabled bodies. While the poem resists this threat by drawing on the figure of the signer to locate all bodies on the spectrum of disability, the conclusion reintroduces the threat by collapsing the spectrum of ability into the homogenised One.

Environment in "Marsh Languages"

Atwood's "Marsh Languages" confirms the threat of the homogenising apocalypse that "The Signer" veils with a gesture of hope. In "Marsh Languages", the unification of language is a colonial move that kills and destroys othered bodies as linguistic difference succumbs to linguistic unity. In "Marsh Languages", language has meaning in vital material, and the separation of life from matter creates a meaninglessness that sets an apocalyptic trajectory.

This poem begins chanting, "The dark soft languages are being silenced / Mothertongue Mothertongue Mothertongue / falling one by one back into the moon". In these lines, the poem both ascribes vitality to matter in the form of language and threatens this ascription by suggesting that this linguistic vitality is being silenced. While the poem does not collapse the difference between human and non-human materials, it evokes emotive connections between humans and non-humans by paralleling the materiality of earth with the materiality of human bodies:

> Language of marshes, / language of the roots of rushes tangled / together in the ooze, / marrow cells twinning themselves / inside the warm core of the bone.

This passage facilitates affective connections for the poem's human audience by introducing the possibility that the non-human world may also feel. As earthy matter and human bodies speak a common language, the poem gives life to vital matter by recognising that the so-called parts may have intents, operations, vitality of their own. While this vitality finds expression in language, the poem maintains that different matters speak different languages: languages of marshes, roots, cave languages, sun languages, languages of the human body.

Because earthy matter does not speak in contemporary discourse (we do not, for example, say 'the moss says'), the poem's ascription of language to matter fails to make sense and forces a reconsideration of language, earthy matter and the relationship between the two. This defamilarisation process forces a reconsideration of the nature of matter and, thus, enacts new materialist calls to attribute vitality to matter we have presumed to be static and inert. According to Jane Bennett, in order to parse through the ways moderns have distinguished between life and matter, we have to turn common uses of these words around and around until they start to seem strange. Such a turning of language can lead to the realisation that matter is vital and alive and challenge linguistic patterns that have screened the vitality of matter from view (vii).

Although the poem may give voice to vitalist theories of matter, each verse ends hinting toward an apocalypse in which vitality is removed from matter and replaced by a unified, binary language. In addition to the languages falling back into the moon and the linguistic pathways that are fading out, the poem describes,

> All are becoming sounds no longer / heard because no longer spoken, / and everything that could once be said in them has / ceased to exist.

In each of these scenes, matter must speak in order to mean, and, as it ceases to speak, it will cease to exist.

This threat that removing language from matter results in death is confirmed when the poem describes how materials have lost their language, "[the mouth] can no longer speak both cherishing and farewell / It is now only a mouth, only skin / There is no more longing". In these images, speech is recentralised not as a logical and grammatically correct sequence of words but as cherishing, farewell and longing. Like the poem's earlier move of attributing language to matter, the poem's attribution of loss to matter creates non-sense in order to facilitate alternative ways of making sense. Non-human matter, thus, not only speaks but also feels, cherishes, longs. In this attribution of speech and emotion to non-human matter, the poem's vital materialism dissolves the binary between human agency and non-human passivity. Rather than screening the vitality of matter from view or reducing agency to human agency, the poem evokes a dynamic image of material that has potential apart from human agency. Thus, the dissociation of language from matter does not reveal the passive, static, inertness of matter as if it were only waiting for a human agent but, rather, demonstrates the deadliness of the human agent who has attempted to deny the vitality of matter and destroyed it in the process. Where there was vital matter, there remains only a mouth, only skin, the modern world and the binary language that mechanises that world.

As in "The Signer", "Marsh Languages" maintains difference by resisting translation, for now, "[translation] was never possible". Like "The Signer", the untranslatable difference becomes reconciled in a unitive, "the one language that has eaten all the others". Yet, unlike "The Signer", the unification of linguistic and bodily difference is not a hopeful gesture, "[instead] there was always only / conquest, the influx / of the language of hard nouns, / the language of metal, / the language of either/or". The violent image of conquest, in which the hard nouns and either/ors replace the sibilants and gutturals, the syllable for I that did not mean separate, and the mothertongue, suggests that the silencing of languages forces bodies into a logic of the same that kills linguistic difference and threatens bodies that fail to enter into the logic of the same. The lost languages carry multiple connotations here: earthy, feminine, non-Western. Here, the present swallows the past and colonises the future by forcing matter's vital diversity into a dogmatic discourse where everything other than the language of separation ceases to exist. The poem describes a scene in which languages are pulled from the bodies that spoke them, ultimately resulting in the dissolution of the link between language and bodies and the deaths of bodies.

On the one hand, by ascribing linguistic agency to matter, the poem challenges anthropocentric discourses that assume either that humans control nature or that humans bear the responsibility of paternalistically caring for nature. On the other hand, by threatening the agency she has ascribed to matter, the poem identifies an agent that may have the potential to reverse the silencing of matter. Although the agent does not appear in the poem, the suggested activities of the agent, activities such as conquest, suggest that the agent is human. The poem thus mitigates the difference between human and non-human by attributing vitality to matter without collapsing the difference.

Like climate change discourses, the poem foresees apocalypse as a result of human interactions with the natural world. Yet the attribution of agency to matter in this poem contains the seeds to arrest the foreseen apocalypse. Attributing agency to materiality works to arrest apocalypse in two ways. First, attributing agency to materiality suggests that the world can reorganise in unexpected ways, thus arresting the apocalyptic future prophesied by climate change discourse if materials speak their own languages. Second, attributing agency to materiality rejects the human/nature binary and demonstrates the inadequacy of modes of language that assume either a domineering or paternalistic relation of humans to nature. The poem thus embodies new materialist understandings of matter, offering ways to link matter and language that press linguistic attempts to capture and control both human and non-human matter.

Gender in "Half-Hanged Mary"

If the hopeful eschatological picture in "The Signer" unites languages and bodies while the pessimistic apocalyptic vision in "Marsh Languages" tears language from bodies, "Half-Hanged Mary" merges these movements. This poem draws on the hanging of Mary Webster in Massachusetts in the 1680s for practices of witchcraft; a hanging Mary survived. In the poem based on this historical account, Atwood frames Mary's experience in light of the hours she hung. These uneven hourly reminders break up the poetic stanzas and serve as a haunting refrain: 7pm, 8pm, 9pm, 10pm, 12 midnight, 2am, 3am, 6am, 8am, Later. In this poem, a patriarchal narrative in the form of a noose successfully disintegrates Mary's body and her voice, but she survives this judgment by both adopting and challenging the patriarchal narrative. Like "Marsh Languages", "Half-Hanged Mary" reveals the bodily violence that results from homogenised narratives. Yet, like "The Signer", a complicated agency develops in this homogenisation of Mary's narrative and the patriarchal narrative, which threatens the patriarchal narrative by entering into it, but not entirely.

The first section explains the circumstances surrounding Mary's hanging, "Rumor was loose in the air, / hunting for some neck to land on. / I was milking the cow, / the barn door open to the sunset". Pairing social complexity in the form of rumours with pastoral simplicity in the form of barns and cows, this stanza gestures toward the speaker's innocence. This innocence is confirmed by the third and fourth stanzas:

> I was hanged for living alone . . . a weedy farm in my own name, / and a surefire cure for warts; / Oh yes, and breasts, / and a sweet pear hidden in my body.

In Atwood's rendition, Mary becomes the target of the force of patriarchal violence, a violence that moves in an apocalyptic arc. Mary's non-normative female body, which refuses to conform to social logic, must be silenced by drawing a loop tight around her neck to prevent air from crossing the vocal cords. Mary's hanging literally silences her. Yet by locating the narrative in Mary's speech, the poem disempowers the rumours, cutting off the justifications of Mary's accusers and arresting the apocalyptic arc created by the patriarchal narrative.

The poem further disempowers the narrative of the accusers by describing how Mary speaks with God while she hangs, "Well God, now that I'm up here . . . we can continue our quarrel . . . Is it my choice that I'm dangling"? By directing the protest that her death is not her choice to God, the speaker implies that the responsible agent for her death is God.

With this reference to the free will debate, the poem locates itself historically in the seventeenth century debates between the followers of John Calvin, who claimed that God intentionally directed the human will to respond to the offer of grace, and Jacob Arminius, who claimed that human beings were free to respond to the offer of God's grace by their own choice. This debate fuels the tension between Mary's self-description, which might be described as that of a free agent, and the rumours the patriarchal narrative writes on her body, which might be described as the Calvinist attempt to inscribe Mary within the divine law and the divine Word. Mary's ability to speak for herself thus threatens the patriarchal narrative, a threat the noose attempts and ultimately fails to subdue.

The following lines develop Mary's protest against Calvinist theologies, "If Nature is Your alphabet, what letter is this rope? / Does my twisting body spell out Grace"? In addition to mocking the Puritan naivety that regards nature as a revelation of God, these lines add the layer of divinity to the relationship between language and bodies developed in "The Signer" and "Marsh Languages". In these words, the poem associates language and bodies by suggesting that there is a connection not only between human language and matter but also between divine language and matter. The poem performs this move, first, by evoking the crucifixion in the twisting body of Mary and, second, by connecting broken bodies with divine Grace. If the crucified body of Jesus effects salvation or "spells out grace", as some Christians maintain, might the hanging body of Mary also spell out grace? In this implied question, the poem challenges Christian narratives both by elevating Mary (Webster) to the divine status of Jesus and by mocking the association of torture and grace in some Christian interpretations of the cross. Both human and divine thus speak and exist in material forms, but the type and shape of the material forms change their language. In these senses, there may be a relationship between God and nature, but the poem presses the question to consider how specific material forms change not only our language but also our understanding of divinity. If divinity is revealed in tortured bodies, what does that suggest about the nature of the divine?

The poem develops the relationship between language and bodies as death haunts Mary in the midnight refrain, "My throat is taut against the rope / choking off words and air; / I'm reduced to knotted muscle". Being no more than a body part, a muscle, Mary sees death sitting on her shoulder and begins to voice his presence instead of hers. As Mary describes Death's words, Death appears to have won as Mary stops speaking and death enters the silence "muttering about sluts and punishment ... whispering to me to be easy / on myself". In this transition from Mary's voice to the voice of Death, Mary's pain threatens her destruction. As Elaine Scarry describes,

> To witness the moment when pain causes a reversion to the pre-language cries and groans is to witness the destruction of language; but, conversely, to be present when a person moves up out of that pre-language and projects the facts of sentience into speech is almost to have been permitted to be present at the birth of language itself. (6)

Pain, according to Scarry, changes the meaning of material bodies, constrains language and threatens their very existence.

While Mary's language may be destroyed as she hangs at midnight, the following stanza breaks Death's hold on language: "Out of my mouth is coming, at some / distance from me, a thin gnawing sound". This sound represents the speaker's fight against death for life, but it is broken, for the speaker is no longer fighting the silence with words but with unconstrained sounds. As Scarry states,

> Though there is no ordinary language for pain, under the pressure of the desire to eliminate pain, an at least fragmentary means of verbalization is available both to those who are themselves in pain and to those who wish to speak on behalf of others. (Scarry 13)

This thin, gnawing sound, a fragmentary means of verbalisation, indicates life but barely. This sound disappears in the 6am refrain in which silence re-enters, as the speaker says, "At the end of my rope / I testify to silence". Again, though, the silence is not final as Mary is cut down in the 8am refrain, "Surprise, surprise: / I was still alive". The interplay between Mary's voice, the voice of death, a voice that fights to make any sound at all, and silence reveals the noose's attempt to silence Mary by destroying her body and her attempt to survive this patriarchal violence. Ultimately, Mary does survive but only because her tortured body takes on a new language. While her body had been subject to judgment because of its incoherence with patriarchal language, her body now both exists within patriarchal language and exceeds that language.

Mary, however, does not immediately demonstrate this life with speech but looks at her accusers, noting, "Before, I was not a witch / But now I am one". In this line, the poem suggests that Mary's torture has forced her body to conform to the patriarchal language. In owning her judgment, the speaker steels herself to survive. As Sarah Ahmed describes, "Sometimes you have to become what you are judged as being to survive that judgment". Mary thus becomes a witch in order to survive the accusation that she was one. Moreover, her confession demonstrates that her previous self has been unmade such that the only way to survive is to adopt the violent language of her accusers. As Scarry notes, "The confession which displays the fact that he has nothing to live for now obscures the fact that he is violently alive" (38). Mary has not been silenced by the patriarchal accusations brought against her or her hanging, but has adopted a new body, "Also, I'm about three inches taller", complete with a new language:

> I skitter over the paths and fields / mumbling to myself like crazy, / mouth full of juicy adjectives / and purple berries . . . I speak in tongues, / my audience is owls.

She speaks, but her language no longer corresponds to the realities of others. The social response confirms this violent existence, "The townsfolk dive headfirst into the bushes / to get out of my way".

The poem concludes with an apocalyptic vision that extends this immediate social analysis into cosmic destruction as the language the speaker speaks unravels the world, "The words boil out of me, / coil after coil of sinuous possibility. / The cosmos unravels from my mouth, / all fullness, all vacancy". Because the speaker maintains that she has been silenced by death only to return from that silence, the resulting integration of life, body and language creates a threatening possibility that presents itself in a resurrected body. By calling attention to resurrection and connecting the speaker with the divine, the poem furthers this interpretive possibility when Mary states, "My audience is God, / because who the hell else could understand me? / Who else has been dead twice"? By weaving the divine into the web of language and bodies, Atwood's apocalypticism takes on a new valence as the disconnection and reconnection of language and bodies divinise the speaker. Having encountered the profound disintegration of language and body by glimpsing her death, the speaker now holds the divine linguistic keys to the ravelling and unravelling of the world. In the deadly disintegration of language and body, a new speech emerges that not only integrates language and body but understands the integration and, therefore, holds the key to its maintenance—and its unravelling.

Conclusion

The conclusion of "Half-Hanged Mary" unites the hope of "The Signer" with the threat of "Marsh Languages" as the speaker describes the life-giving unification of language and bodies and the death-dealing dissolution of language and bodies, a description that offers promise and dread. In these poetic accounts, Atwood's poems suggest that apocalypse uses alternating gestures of fear and hope to mobilise us for present actions that value bodies and their particular languages. In particular, Atwood's attention to marginalised bodies demonstrates the value of linguistic multiplicity as a key to arresting apocalypse.

These poems suggest that valuing bodies requires creating spaces in which bodies can speak without being homogenised into the logic of the Same. A singular language, in other words, threatens to kill and subdue bodies by inscribing them into a unifying logic. Multiple languages, on the other hand, create space for the existence of multiple bodies, allowing multiple bodies to speak their own lives. Yet, as "Half-Hanged Mary" demonstrates, even in systems that demand homogenisation by killing any threat to that homogenisation, an excess emerges, which distorts the homogenised language and creates space for new life to emerge within the unifying logic and the violence it perpetuates. These poems therefore not only describe apocalypse but also contain the seeds to arrest apocalypse.

The languages are being silenced by ableism, environmental degradation and patriarchy. If these are allowed to continue, Atwood's poems suggest that apocalypse will result. Rather than resigning to this apocalyptic arc, Atwood attempts to describe it in order to arrest it. In this sense, Atwood's poetic descriptions of the apocalyptic arc function to prevent the forthcoming apocalypse. By reuniting the languages that ableism, environmental degradation and patriarchy have pulled from bodies to those bodies from which they have been pulled, Atwood's poems suggest that the key to arresting the impending apocalypse is to restore language to bodies, especially marginalised bodies.

Works Cited

Ahmed, Sara (SaraNAhmed). "Sometimes: you have to become what you are judged as being to survive that judgment". 30 March 2014, 6:16 a.m. Tweet.

Atwood, Margaret. *Morning in the Burned House*. New York: Houghton Mifflin, 1996. Print.

—. "The Road to Ustopia". *The Guardian* 14 October 2011. Web. 18 April 2014.

Bennett, Jane. *Vibrant Matter: A Political Ecology of Things*. Durham and London: Duke University Press, 2010. Print.

Betcher, Sharon V. *Spirit and the Politics of Disablement*. Minneapolis: Fortress Press, 2007. Print.

Scarry, Elaine. *The Body in Pain: The Making and Unmaking of the World*. New York: Oxford University, 1985. Print.

Siebers, Tobin. *Disability Theory*. Ann Arbor: University of Michigan, 2008. Print.

Thill, Scott. "Margaret Atwood, Speculative Fiction's Apocalyptic Optimist". *Wired*. 20 October 2009. Web. 18 April 2014.

CHAPTER THREE

SUICIDE AS APOCALYPSE
IN *THE HANDMAID'S TALE*

PATRICIA A. STAPLETON

When addressing the concept of "apocalypse" in literature, we are required to define its usage. Narrowly defined, apocalypse means complete annihilation, the literal end of the world. Post-apocalyptic texts, therefore, are problematic because they envision a world after the end. Clearly though, there are fictional narratives that proceed after near-apocalyptic events. James Berger supplies a useful frame for addressing this issue, by defining apocalypse as potentially occurring at three different levels: world, society and individual. In Margaret Atwood's *The Handmaid's Tale*, we see all three definitions at play; fears about the actual end of the world have led to an apocalypse in American society and in the life of the main character Offred. Under the guise of threats to humanity, a holy war has been launched, and Offred has been conscripted and re-educated as a Handmaid to serve the reproductive needs of the elite.

Offred's life as she knew it—her family, her marriage, her career and her freedom—has been destroyed. Life as Americans have known it is completely upended. Yet, while the reader comes to learn many of the details of Offred's life before and during these apocalyptic times, the end of her story remains ambiguous. However, Atwood has provided several clues throughout the text so that readers can reconstruct Offred's end, similar to how the conference scholars included in the epilogue to the text have reconstructed the narrative.

These clues develop as three parallel frames to Offred's story: the fate of the handmaid, also named Offred, who preceded the Offred that the reader comes to know; the role of Offred's companion Ofglen in the resistance; and the interview with the Nazi mistress that appears in one of Offred's recollections. All three frames establish the trajectory of Offred's story. But it is the third frame—that of the Nazi mistress—that reveals the true end of *The Handmaid's Tale*. Like the Nazi mistress, Offred is telling her story for posterity. And it is through her own retelling that Offred comes to recognise her complicity in atrocity, like the Nazi mistress. Thus, the recounted TV interview unlocks Offred's story, revealing that Offred commits suicide after she has completed her recordings.

Although located in apocalyptic times, it is Offred's suicide that is the apocalyptic event of the novel: the literal end to Offred herself. Yet Offred's suicide is not simply a desperate or depressive attempt at escape. While the retelling of her story may reflect feelings of guilt and complicity, her suicide is also a way for Offred to take control of the narrative and her own body again. The ultimate act of killing herself is a revelation; it allows Offred the power to stop her story when she—and no one else—has decided.

Berger's definitions of apocalypse

Berger locates his discussion of apocalypse in the context of trauma, which he argues is the psychoanalytic term for apocalypse (20). He explores "the idea of post-apocalypse, of modes of expression made in the wake of catastrophes so overwhelming that they seem to negate the possibility of expression at the same time that they compel expression" (5). This vision tracks well with the narrative of *The Handmaid's Tale*, which is recounted through different modes of expression during a time when the possibility of expression through writing—forbidden for Handmaids—has been negated.

More importantly, Berger provides a framework for understanding apocalyptic texts, which almost universally present the same paradox: "The end is never the end" (5). To do so, he presents "apocalypse" in three senses:

> First, it is the *eschaton*, the actual imagined end of the world, as presented in the New Testament Apocalypse... or as imagined... today in visions of nuclear Armageddon or ecological suicide. Second, apocalypse refers to catastrophes that resemble the imagined final ending, that can be interpreted as eschaton, as an end of something, a way of life or thinking... [I]n our age the Holocaust and the use of atomic weapons against the Japanese have assumed apocalyptic significance. They function as definitive historical divides, as ruptures... separating what came before from what came after... Apocalypse, thus, finally, has an interpretative, explanatory function, which is, of course, its etymological sense: as revelation, unveiling, uncovering. (Berger 5)

In this way, Berger supplies definitions for apocalypse at different levels: worldwide destruction; society-wide devastation; and individual obliteration.

In *The Handmaid's Tale*, all three senses are at play. Fears of the actual end of the world, due to declining rates of fertility and environmental degradation, threaten humanity. These fears are used as the justification for the society-wide apocalypse that is occurring through the medium of civil war. The holy war being waged has created an historical rupture, demarcating the pre-Gileadean period and the current era. More specifically, the narrator of the tale, Offred, remembers the freedoms and independence afforded women in the time before. This way of life has ended, and women are now under the complete control of men.

It is Berger's apocalypse in the third sense, however, that provides the most insight into the experience of Offred. The idea of apocalypse as revelation occurs at an individual level. But it is not any uncovering that rises to the level of apocalypse; the revelation must be traumatic at the same time that it is enlightening. Berger clarifies that, in the third sense,

> [t]he apocalyptic event, in order to be properly apocalyptic, must in its destructive moment clarify and illuminate the true nature of what has been brought to an end. (5)

Applied to Offred, it is through the recounting of her experience that her complicity becomes illuminated. In addition, as her narrative unfolds, she must also come to terms with the loss of her agency. By destroying herself, Offred is able to bring to an end her complicit participation in Gileadean society and to reclaim her autonomy.

Suicide in post-apocalyptic narratives

Suicide in post-apocalyptic narratives is not uncommon. In the chaotic or disorienting environment of a fictional new world order, characters often opt out. For some, like the woman in Cormac McCarthy's *The Road*, suicide seems to be the only way to avoid an excruciating end. For others, like John the Savage in Aldous Huxley's *Brave New World*, it is a way to remove oneself from a world that the individual no longer understands. These two literary examples provide a backdrop for understanding Offred's suicide in *The Handmaid's Tale*.

McCarthy never explains the details of the apocalyptic event, only the aftermath, as the man and the boy restlessly roam. But the "cauterized terrain" (14), ashen, grainy and raw seems to be the result of nuclear holocaust. The man remembers:

> The clocks stopped at 1:17. A long shear of light and then a series of low concussions... A dull rose glow in the windowglass. (McCarthy 52)

In the initial years following, refugees wandered the roads in "masks and goggles" (McCarthy 28). The landscape through which the man and the boy pass is blackened by fires, though cold and barren, devoid of living vegetation or wildlife.

In *The Road*'s dystopian future, humans are nearing extinction—a literal apocalypse. Food is scarce, and the environment is harsh. Any social mores have long disappeared, and the gangs of people that remain appear to survive on human flesh. Confronted with the inevitably of the pain and suffering of their life of wandering, the woman (the wife of the man and mother of the boy) decides to commit suicide. The man tries to convince the woman to stay, arguing that they are survivors (McCarthy 55) and that she is talking crazy (McCarthy 56). But the woman fights back:

> No, I'm speaking the truth. Sooner or later they will catch us and they will kill us. They will rape me. They'll rape him. They are going to rape us and kill us and eat us and you won't face it. You'd rather wait for it to happen. But I can't. I can't. (McCarthy 56)

The man knows how she will kill herself and recognises that she is right; her decision is an enlightened one:

> There was no argument. The hundred nights they'd sat up debating the pros and cons of self destruction with the earnestness of philosophers chained to a madhouse wall. (McCarthy 58)

The woman walks off into the dark to take her own life, leaving her husband and son behind. Her suicide is certainly an act of desperation, yet her choice is simply the manner of her demise; she has no options for avoiding it. Rather than waiting to have the apocalyptic world act on her, the woman wilfully chooses her death. For the woman, she is regaining some control over a life that has been upended. While death is always inevitable, the woman chooses how and when she will leave the world, instead of waiting to be tortured, raped, murdered and cannibalised. The woman's act is the result of bleak options, but it allows the woman to recover some control over her own body and narrative in the chaos.

The final scenes of *Brave New World* reveal a similar theme. The modern world into which John the Savage has been inserted does not make sense to him. His final conversations with Controller Mustapha Mond and with his friends, before he attempts to detach himself from modern society, reveal his feelings. In response to Mond's insistence that this world was a better version than the time before, John catalogues all that is missing:

> "But I like inconveniences."
> "We don't," said the Controller. "We prefer to do things comfortably."
> "But I don't want comfort. I want God, I want poetry, I want real danger, I want freedom, I want goodness. I want sin."
> "In fact," said Mustapha Mond, "you're claiming the right to be unhappy."
> "Alright then," said the Savage defiantly, "I'm claiming the right to be unhappy." …
> "I claim them all," said the Savage at last. (Huxley 215)

John is claiming the right to live his life as he wants, not in a way that is predetermined by society. Society, as the modern elite envision it, is not agreeable to him: "'Did you eat something that didn't agree with you?' asked Bernard. The Savage nodded. 'I ate civilization'" (Huxley 216).

Acknowledging that he has no place in this social experiment, the Savage retreats to an abandoned lighthouse, where he thinks that he can isolate himself from the corrupting influences of the immoral world and atone for his sins through discipline, purges and self-flagellation. Of course, his isolation does not last, as the world will not leave him in peace. The culmination of John's story is world-shattering for him; he gives in to temptation to the utmost degree, participating in a soma-fuelled orgy, awakening the next morning ashamed and unmoored:

> [The Savage] lay for a moment, blinking in owlish incomprehension at the light; then suddenly remembered—everything. 'Oh, my God, my God!' He covered his eyes with his hand. (Huxley 230)

When eager revellers return that evening to repeat the debauched spectacle, they find the Savage hanging, dead by his own hand.

John's suicide illustrates two themes. One, like the woman in *The Road*, the suicide allows John to recover his autonomy. This brave new world is not a world he can ever come to accept, and he is doomed to a life determined at its mercy. However, he has also succumbed to the sins of the modern world, and consequently he must be penitent. Thus, the second theme is that John's suicide allows him to exorcise his complicity in the orgy. Not only did he participate, but he enjoyed it. And, for that, John must show that he repents.

There is also another element of John the Savage's suicide that can provide insight into Offred's story. His participation in the orgy does not immediately precipitate his suicide; rather, it is the act of remembering that drives him to kill himself. John's recollection of what has happened and his role in it, when seen in the light of day, destroys him.

Offred's Story

Although other dystopian, post-apocalyptic texts offer examples of how to read the theme of suicide, Atwood provides her own signs for the reader to understand Offred's fate. However, in order to be recognisable, the text must be reread. Atwood's "Historical Notes on *The Handmaid's Tale*" at the end of the text is a direct invitation to rethink the narrative. In the epilogue, it becomes clear that, in a future era over one hundred and fifty years after Offred's life, scholars have reconstructed this work from cassette tapes. Offred's tale is actually a recorded oral narrative, but the cassettes were not preserved in their original order. Instead, a male scholar, Professor Pieixoto, has pieced together her tale to present at an academic conference.

However, as Hogsette notes, this ending is ironic because "it provides readers with an example of how not to read Atwood's novel…" (263). Over the course of the novel, Atwood has presented "the reader with the limited perspective of a woman trapped in the oppressive, patriarchal society of the Republic of Gilead" (Hogsette 264), and the "Historical Notes" create a disruption to feminist readings of the text because of Professor Pieixoto's "chauvinistic misreading" (Hogsette 265). As a result,

> Atwood's novel begins—with the handmaid's narrative—exploring silence and speech, oppression and resistance. The novel ends—with a male scholar's narrative—questioning the limits of narrative and interpretation. (Stein 270)

Yet, once knowing that the narrative has been reconstructed, the reader can return to the text to reread it and reconsider its construction. In doing so, the reader can find the clues left by Atwood that not only restore the feminist context to the tale, but also restore agency to Offred.

Despite the Gileadean elite's best efforts to strip women of physical autonomy, in the novel there is still a pervasive fear that the Handmaids will commit suicide. The new leadership's concern is that women will be desperate to opt-out of their coerced sexual enslavement, resulting in the loss of a potential national resource: a fertile woman. As a result, Handmaids do not have access to items that they might use to harm themselves, like glass (the removal of mirrors, the installation of safety windows, etc.) or sharp objects (knives, scissors, etc.). They are also denied access to opportunity: they are rarely left alone, and even their time in the bathroom is closely guarded. In this new society, women's bodies have been re-established as under the complete control of men.

In addition to frequent oblique references to harming oneself, suicide explicitly appears several times in Atwood's text: in the fates of the previous Offred, of the companion Ofglen, and of the interviewed Nazi mistress. If the narrative reconstructed through the male gaze is exactly how *not* to read Offred's story, then these three narratives of other women experiencing apocalyptic times act as maps of how to read it correctly. Atwood creates obvious links between details of the narrator Offred and each of these women, such as distinct gestures, physical characteristics and circumstances. All are mistresses in times of war. All are stripped of their given names, instead marked and remembered only by their associations to powerful men in malevolent forces. And the suicides of all these women are clearly linked to these associations. From the male perspective then, these women are interchangeable.

Handmaids' names were "patronymic, composed of the possessive preposition and the first name of the gentleman in question" (Atwood 305). As a result, the handmaid that was assigned to Offred's Commander would have always been designated "Of-Fred". Thus, in terms of linkages between the two characters, not only did the previous Offred have the same name as the narrator, but she also occupied the same physical space and position within the household. Over the course of the story, the reader discovers along with the narrator that the previous Offred has occupied the position of mistress to the Commander too. The previous Offred has even left her replacement what seems like a maxim to live by, but turns out to be a warning: *Nolite te bastardes carborundorum* [don't let the bastards grind you down] (Atwood 52, 187). By inscribing the words into the bedroom cupboard, the previous Offred has left a clue:

> I can see why she wrote that, on the wall of the cupboard, but I also see that she must have learned it here, in this room... I have not been the first then.
> "What happened to her?" I say...
> "She hanged herself," [the Commander] says; thoughtfully, not sadly. "That's why we had the light fixture removed. In your room." He pauses. "Serena found out," he says, as if it explains it. And it does...

> Things have changed. I have something on him, now. What I have on him
> is the possibility of my own death. (Atwood 187-188)

In this scene, the narrator acknowledges how she can be easily
interchanged with her predecessor, which also means that she too could
opt-out.

The scene in which Serena Joy confronts the narrator Offred about her
night "out" with the Commander further reinforces this linkage:

> "Look," [Serena Joy] says. She brings her free hand from behind her back.
> It's her cloak she's holding, the winter one. "There was lipstick on it," she
> says. "How could you be so vulgar? I *told* him…" She drops the cloak,
> she's holding something else, her hand all bone. She throws that down as
> well. The purple sequins fall, slithering down over the step like snakeskin,
> glittering in the sunlight. … "Pick up that disgusting thing and get to your
> room. Just like the other one. A slut. You'll end up the same." (Atwood
> 287)

Although Serena Joy means dead, the reader can interpret Atwood's intent
also as "dead by your own hand". Like the Offred before, she has been
outed, most likely by the Commander for her complicity (but lack of
eagerness) in his subversion. While Serena Joy may have accidentally
found her own cloak out of place, the discovery of the feathered costume
that the Commander made Offred wear to the hotel raises more suspicion.
After being sent to her room, Offred contemplates the meagre options she
has before her:

> There are a number of things I could do. …I could noose the bedsheet
> around my neck, hook myself up in the closet, throw my weight forward,
> choke myself off. (Atwood 292)

It is here that Atwood connects the narrator and her predecessor the most
clearly:

> Behind me I feel her presence, my ancestress, my double, turning in midair
> under the chandelier, in her costume of stars and feathers, a bird stopped in
> flight, a woman made into an angel, waiting to be found. By me this time.
> How could I have believed I was alone in here? There were always two of
> us. Get it over, she says. I'm tired of this melodrama, I'm tired of keeping
> silent. There's no one you can protect, your life has value to no one. I want
> it finished. (293)

As Offred stands up to follow in the footsteps of her predecessor, the Eyes arrive to take her away.

It is this scene that alerts the reader to a clear connection between Offred and Ofglen as well. Offred is told by the "new" Ofglen that her former shopping companion has committed suicide: "'She hanged herself,' she says. 'After the Salvaging. She saw the van coming for her. It was better'" (Atwood 285). Consequently, as Offred awaits judgment in the same way that Ofglen and the previous Offred did, she endures the image of her double hanging not once, but twice over.

Prior to Offred's final scene at the Commander's home, Atwood has already established other similarities between Offred and her shopping companion. Ofglen is the mirror-version of Offred, from the first moment they meet: "A shape, red with white wings around the face, a shape like mine, a nondescript woman in red carrying a basket..." (Atwood 19). The mirror imagery repeats in the text: "Doubled, I walk the street" (Atwood 23), "I watch her. She's like my own reflection, in a mirror from which I am moving away" (Atwood 45) and "...we're used to each other. Siamese twins" (Atwood 165). Atwood even describes Offred and Ofglen as moving and thinking in tandem when out on their walks: "We turn the corner" (24); "...we wait in our double line", "We hand over our tokens", "We put [the purchases] into our baskets and go out again" (26); "We are fascinated, but also repelled" (28); and "We stop, together as if on signal..." (32).

Where they diverge is their support of the resistance; Ofglen is an active member of the Mayday operation, but Offred fails to use her access to the Commander to any kind of advantage. She even feels relief when Ofglen appears to give up on Offred helping the resistance (Atwood 271). At first, when Offred finds out that Ofglen has committed suicide, and therefore cannot possibly inform on her, Offred is flooded with relief. Perhaps more tellingly, however, she is also flooded with a desire to be utterly submissive:

> Dear God, I think, I will do anything you like. Now that you've let me off, I'll obliterate myself, if that's what you really want; I'll empty myself, truly, become a chalice ... I know this can't be right but I think it anyway. Everything they taught at the Red Center, everything I've resisted, comes flooding in. I don't want to feel pain. I don't want to be a dancer, my feet in the air, my head a faceless oblong of white cloth. I don't want to be a doll hung up on the Wall, I don't want to be a wingless angel. I want to keep on living, in any form. I resign my body freely, to the uses of others. They can do what they like with me. I am abject. I feel, for the first time, their true power. (Atwood 286)

Offred thinks that she can offer up her own bodily autonomy in a bargain with God for her life. Even still, she mistakenly believes that her choices are between being used freely by others and being killed by others. In the following scenes where she is confronted by Serena Joy and the ghost of her predecessor, Offred finds another way: she can reclaim her autonomy and her body by taking her life.

The manner of suicide by both Offred's predecessor and Ofglen further reinforces suicide as a reclaimative act. If taken by the Eyes, the women would be tortured for information and then publically hanged. Although Offred does not want to be "a wingless angel" hanging on the Wall, she is prepared to become "a woman made into an angel" like her double. She intends to reclaim her autonomy. Like the mother in *The Road*, the Handmaids are faced with a desperate choice: physical violation and certain death at the hands of others, or death by their own. By committing suicide, a Handmaid thus makes a powerful statement: she would rather take her own life than submit to Gileadean judgment. Apocalyptic enlightenment is achieved when Offred realises that to not be "ground down" means to retake control, to subvert the power of the bastards by reclaiming her physical autonomy.

Like the other Handmaids' tales, the story of the Nazi mistress is a narrative nested within a narrative, which, readers find out at the end of the book, is nested in yet another narrative. Offred's larger narrative has been reconstructed by future scholars, like the story of the Nazi mistress. But while all of the Handmaids' stories unfold in the Republic of Gilead with brief recollections of the pre-Gileadean era, the Nazi mistress is from a time long before. Atwood provides the documentary interview of the Nazi mistress as an illustration of how to read Offred's tale with historical perspective. The memory of watching it is introduced with Offred's avowal that "Context is all" for understanding her experience (Atwood 144). Offred recalls her mother explaining that such terrible things had really happened in the past, but Offred only recognises the World War II documentary as a story:

> I thought someone had made it up. I suppose all children think that, about any history before their own. If it's only a story, it becomes less frightening. (Atwood 144)

The documentary includes an interview with "a woman who had been the mistress of a man who had supervised one of the camps where they put the Jews, before they killed them" (Atwood 145). Offred remembers,

> From what they said, the man had been cruel and brutal … The woman said she didn't notice much that she found unusual. She denied knowing about the ovens… He was not a monster, she said. People say he was a monster, but he was not one. (Atwood 145)

What Offred remembers most about the interview is the mistress's pride in her appearance and her attempts to humanise the Nazi commander (Atwood 145, 146). Offred performs these same acts of pride and humanisation with her Commander. She also remembers the addendum to the documentary: the mistress committed suicide days after her interview.

Atwood makes a more direct link between the Nazi documentary and Offred in the scene at Jezebel's:

> He's stroking my body now… He stops at the foot, his fingers encircling the ankle, briefly, like a bracelet, where the tattoo is, a Braille he can read, a cattle brand. It means ownership. (254)

Still, even in that moment of coerced sex where he deliberately reminds her of his power over her body, Offred tries to humanise him: "I remind myself that he is not an unkind man; that, under other circumstances, I even like him… He is not a monster, I think" (Atwood 254, 255). But the Commander is a monster; he is playing the same games with her that he did with her predecessor. And those games led directly to the death of the previous Offred. But in the moment—in that context—Offred needs to convince herself that he was not cruel and brutal in order to survive.

However, once she has escaped and has the distance (mentally and physically) from her experience, she must face not only the Commander's insidious brutality, but also her complicity. Like the Nazi mistress, Offred is ignorant or in denial of her complicity during the experience—a necessary survival tactic. In recounting her story, though, the Nazi mistress must unveil her role in the atrocities committed or, at the least, in her lack of action to do something about those atrocities. Although she was not directly involved in the extermination of the Jews, the mistress profited from the power and status of her lover. As a result, her suicide is like John the Savage's: penance for receiving the fruits of sin.

But her suicide also reveals the mistress's fear of shame brought by a society that does not recognise the coercion of women into these acts by powerful men. While the fates of the previous Offred and Ofglen provide context for the narrator's experience, it is the Nazi mistress who provides the final clue to Offred's true end. Once the story has been told, and the narrator must account for the moments of complicity through inaction, there is nothing left. Through recounting their tales, whether the Nazi mistress or the Gileadean mistress, the narrators must come to terms with their lack of resistance. As Offred notes, context is all, and history does not judge fairly. Both mistresses must know how they look to others; Offred even anticipates that she will not be heard: "I'll pretend you can hear me. But it's no good, because I know you can't" (Atwood 40).

In telling her story, Offred has tried to provide the context to her narrative. But the reader sees in the epilogue that her experience is not properly understood and the context is lost. Her narrative is pieced together by a man, who ignores the possibility of her own bodily autonomy, who ignores the clues throughout that point to her suicide and who apologises for the behaviour of the Gileadean male elite. Atwood leaves markers to indicate that Offred comes to this realisation as her tale unfolds. Her experience will later become a "story", but it is not a story to her:

> I would like to believe this is a story I'm telling. I need to believe it. I must believe it. Those who can believe that such stories are only stories have a better chance.
> If it's a story I'm telling, then I have control over the ending. Then there will be an ending, to the story, and real life will come after it. I can pick up where I left off.
> It isn't a story I'm telling. (Atwood 39)

What Offred has told is not a story, but a recollection of historical experience. Yet history will not be kind to her, and her narrative will not be understood. Despite Offred's belief that one plus one plus one plus one does not equal four and that people are not interchangeable (Atwood 192), the reader sees that, for men, individuals are interchangeable (Atwood 186): Offred for Offred, Ofglen for Ofglen, mistress for mistress, woman for woman. Future scholars cannot identify her; Offred's narrative becomes the common handmaid's tale.

Once her story is out, and she understands how it may be interpreted or reimagined by others, Offred must regain control of the narrative. There can be no "picking up" where she left off; there can be no return to the time before. To reclaim her autonomy and to atone for her complicity, Offred takes her own life. Thus, Offred's suicide works as an apocalyptic event on both the societal—and individual—levels. It clarifies and illuminates what has been brought to an end: male control over her body and her life.

Works Cited

Atwood, Margaret. *The Handmaid's Tale.* New York: First Anchor Books Edition, 1998. Print.

Berger, James. *After the End: Representations of Post-Apocalypse.* Minneapolis: University of Minnesota Press, 1999. Print.

Hogsette, David S. "Margaret Atwood's Rhetorical Epilogue in *The Handmaid's Tale*: The Reader's Role in Empowering Offred's Speech Act". *Critique: Studies in Contemporary Fiction* 38.4 (1997): 262-78. Web. 15 Aug. 2010.

Huxley, Aldous. *Brave New World and Brave New World Revisited.* New York: Harper Perennial, 2005. Print.

McCarthy, Cormac. *The Road.* New York: Vintage International, 2006. Print.

Stein, Karen F. "Margaret Atwood's *The Handmaid's Tale:* Scheherazade in Dystopia". *University of Toronto Quarterly* 61.2 (1992): 269-79. Web. 15 Aug. 2010.

CHAPTER FOUR

RESTORING THE DIVINE WITHIN: THE INNER APOCALYPSE IN MARGARET ATWOOD'S *THE YEAR OF THE FLOOD*[1]

ANNA LINDHÉ

So of course we should try to make things better, insofar as it lies within our power. But we should probably not try to make things perfect, especially not ourselves, for that path leads to mass graves. We're stuck with us, imperfect as we are; but we should make the most of us. Which is about as far as I myself am prepared to go, in real life, along the road to ustopia. (Atwood *In Other Worlds* 95)

. . . being flooded with the Light of God's Creation. (Atwood *Year* 43)

Yes, she thought, laying down her brush in extreme fatigue, I have had my vision. (Woolf 151)

That Margaret Atwood's latest novel, *MaddAddam: A Novel* (2013), portrays a utopian world in the otherwise so dystopian *MaddAddam* trilogy (2003-2013) seems evident. At the very end of the book when the close-knit group of previous Madaddamites and Gardeners unite with the pigoons (pigs with human tissue) to rid the newly founded colony of evil, a brighter and more harmonious future seems before them. The pre-apocalyptic landscape of human corruption, perversion and exploitation has been radically transformed to harbour a peaceful posthuman race who lives in harmony with the natural world. The Crakers are not only beautiful and compassionate creatures who are free from disease and notions of romantic love and jealousy; they also feed on grass, leaves and roots, and

---

[1] This paper is based on a paper "Religion and Redemption in Margaret Atwood's *Cat's Eye* and *The Year of the Flood*", presented at the Modern Language Association in Boston in 2013.

possess other features that are harmless to the planet and to themselves. Like in any apocalyptic narrative, then, we witness "the passing away of a degenerate world and the dawning of a new one" in which "[those] who remain will go on to forge a new destiny in a renewed landscape" (Croteau 15). All is well that ends well.

However, this new world—radically altered—is not for us. Crake's ("the mad scientist") revamping of humanity may have saved the planet—stopped the rapid progression towards cataclysm—but it will not save us. In the end is my beginning, T.S. Eliot once confidently wrote, but Atwood's ending is not *our* beginning. At the end of the trilogy, the pen is handed over to (one of) the Crakers. It is their story now, and, in that story, humanity seems beyond redemption and transformation. The post-apocalyptic landscape is thus not a new beginning for *us* but is more likely the end of the human race as we know it. As Gerry Canavan puts it:

> To the extent that Crake's murderous, Frankensteinian actions do indeed usher in a kind of utopia, then, we must understand that it is not a Utopia for *us*—not for us the way we now are, the way we now live. (154)

Still, Atwood's trilogy does offer some kind of hope for us. The utopic core of the trilogy is not, however, located in "earthly" apocalypse but within ourselves, in our potential for transformation. This transformative power—or what is here referred to as the *inner apocalypse*—is activated in the pivotal scene in *The Year of the Flood* (2009), namely in Adam One's rescue of Toby, one of the trilogy's central characters, from the hands of her persecutor, Blanco. This experience radically transforms Toby from victim to redeemer and sets her off in another direction than the path towards despair. Toby's restorative work for God's Gardeners—the eco-religious group whose goal is the redemption of God's creation—bespeaks the power of the individual to transform herself for the benefit of the Other: the planet and all the living things on it. For, to restore harmony with the natural world as well as healthy social relations, humanity, Atwood suggests, needs to restore the divine within, or those ethical aspects of human life, which have somehow been lost: the caring other-oriented emotions of gratitude, charity, forgiveness and love. This essay will demonstrate that Toby's inner apocalypse, prompted by Adam One's rescue, holds out the possibility of a different road, not only for the principal heroine in the trilogy but also for us.

Apocalypse, Utopia and Dystopia

In the biblical book of Revelation, St John of Padmus prophesies the extinction of the human race, which will usher in the kingdom of Christ on earth, a New Jerusalem that will see good prevail over evil. With its end-of-the-world premise—its allusion to Noah's flood, to destruction *and* restoration—Margaret Atwood's trilogy invokes the biblical apocalyptic narrative. The dystopian *before* gives way to a utopian *after*: the kingdom of Crake on earth, which will be carried forward by the Crakers. However, some thinkers would object to the possibility of imagining utopia in the late 20th century and early 21st century,[2] hypothesising that the postmodern tendency towards indifference and pessimism has kicked utopia out forever or at least, as Dale Knickerbocker muses, "made it increasingly difficult to conceive of what a utopia might look like" (347). And, indeed, the society that arises after the apocalypse is not necessarily a utopia or a "better society". Not only, as was hinted at above, does the ending appear dystopian to the human race, there is also reason to believe that the Crakers are on their way to develop the same kind of "imperfections"—curiosity, religion, art, knowledge of their own immortality—that Crake tried to erase. The ambivalent ending of the trilogy reflects the uncertain and indeterminate benefits of the apocalyptic event—the man-made viral plague that the Gardeners call the "Waterless Flood"—and seems to reinforce the idea that utopia is no longer possible.

However, as Dunja Mohr points out, "a disguised literary utopia is very much alive and kicking" in "contemporary literary dystopias" (6),[3] but it may not be as flagrant as that envisioned by Thomas More's who, with his *Utopia* (1516), gave birth to a term as well as a whole genre. Rather, it seems more apt to speak about a "Utopian impulse" than a "Utopian program" in relation to Margaret Atwood's speculative fiction.[4] Many critics have in fact perceived utopian strands or hints of hope in *Oryx and*

---

[2] According to Peter Fitting, "Social upheaval and the negative reactions to the prospect of socialism at the dawn of the twentieth century played an important role in the turn from utopia..." (139).

[3] See also Atwood, who has coined the term "ustopia" to account for the idea that each utopia contains a "concealed dystopia" and each dystopia "a hidden utopia" (*In Other Worlds* 85).

[4] Jameson discerns "two distinct lines of descendency from More's inaugural text: the one intent on the realization of the Utopian program, the other an obscure yet omnipresent Utopian impulse finding its way to the surface in a variety of covert expression and practices" (3).

Crake and *The Year of the Flood*.[5] Mohr detects "utopian glimpses" in language itself: for Snowman/Jimmy in *Oryx and Crake*, "poetic discourse and the remnants of language to which he clings offer redemption and the means for (psychological) survival and hope" (19 and 18). J. Brooks Bouson isolates "a space for utopian hope and desire" in the closure of *The Year of the Flood* (24), and Gerry Canavan identifies utopian possibilities in the apocalyptic break in *Oryx and Crake* and *The Year of the Flood*:

> the core of its unexpectedly utopian politics, lies...in this reopening of possibility: the assertion of the radical break, the strident insistence that things might yet be otherwise. (156)

Canavan is on to something important when he suggests that the apocalypse

> seems to have the capacity to shake the foundations of the system and "jumpstart" a history that now seems completely moribund—the only power left that could still create a renewed, free space in which another kind of life might be possible. (139)

Indeed, the apocalyptic event in Atwood's trilogy puts a rapid end to the evil system and simultaneously makes possible another—more sustainable, it seems—kind of life, but it occurs at the cost of almost the entire human race. Rather than locating the utopian core of the trilogy in the power of the "waterless flood", this essay directs our attention to another powerful "flood" with far less destructive consequences for humanity. Toby's redemptive experience—also described in terms of a flood—of "being *flooded* with the Light of God's Creation" (*Year* 43, emphasis added)—suggests that the power that can "shake the foundations of the system" lies *within* and promises the continuation rather than the annihilation of the human race. The road to utopia, or "ustopia" to use Atwood's own term,[6] begins with Toby's radical break from oppression.

Descending and Rising

Any reader familiar with Atwood's work knows that she often portrays (victimised) women who are or feel trapped and imprisoned, either psychologically in destructive emotions of shame and guilt and/or physically in negative relationships from which they seek to release

---

[5] See also Rozelle.
[6] See Atwood, *In Other Worlds* (66-96).

themselves. This desire to liberate themselves often takes them downwards. In *Surfacing* (1972), the unnamed protagonist is driven to despair over an abortion. In order to free herself from the guilt that is associated with the memories of the abortion, she escapes to the wilderness, where she dives into a lake, "blue and cool as redemption" (11). In *The Edible Woman* (1976), Marian descends into "madness", and Elaine in *Cat's Eye* (1988) descends into her past to rid the emotions of shame and guilt that are attached to the memories of her childhood friend and bully, Cordelia.[7]

The trope of descent[8] is often used in Atwood's fiction to describe the heroine's journey into (and eventually out of) a state of suffering, and *The Year of the Flood* is no exception. Toby's father's sudden suicide has left her with debts towards the Corporation (the private security force, the Corporate Security Corps that controls everything and everyone) that she cannot pay, and, to avoid these, Toby descends into one of the worse pleebs, the Sewage Lagoon. Toby's need to escape the big corporate creditor takes her "*deep down—down* where names disappeared and no histories were true [where] the CorpsSeCorps wouldn't bother with you" (*Year* 30, emphasis added) only to end up in another "debt", as we will see below.

The Pleeblands is a ghetto dominated by an exchange mentality where the (male) inhabitants are free to engage in all kinds of debaucheries.[9] Here, humankind's basest desires and wishes can be gratified often over the bodies of women. But both women and men literally become meat:

> The secret of SecretBurgers was that no one knew what sort of animal protein was actually in them…The meat grinders weren't 100 per cent efficient; you might find a swatch of cat fur in your burger or a fragment of mouse tail. Was there a human fingernail, once? (*Year* 33)

Human beings have become consumer goods themselves, and thus the link between cannibalism and consumer society that runs through Atwood's work is here (Bouson 12), as would be expected of a satire or a dystopia, taken to its extreme. However exaggerated, the distorted images of human

---

[7] Elaine's trip back to Toronto for her retrospective exhibition in *Cat's Eye* is understood in terms of a descent: "I do not rise, I descend", she says (13).

[8] See also Tolan (34n75).

[9] According to Theodore Scheckels, "exchanges characterize the society Atwood has created in *The Year of the Flood*. Those exchanges involve both the small and the large" (156).

relations still serve as a frightening but true mirror to the system of consumption and domination.

Survival is another familiar theme in Atwood's work, and, to survive in *The Year of the Flood*, Toby must paradoxically become someone's "meat". The job she gets at SecretBurgers involves another kind of service apart from serving burgers: she must offer herself to Blanco, the manager of the food chain and the principal villain in the book. The image of a naked woman "wound in chains, her head invisible" inscribed on Blanco's back is supposed to demonstrate that Toby belongs to him. She has no choice but to agree to subservience: "'cross me up, I'll snap you like a twig,' he said" (*Year* 37). Toby has nowhere to go and is thus at the mercy of Blanco, who is in a twisted sense both her persecutor and her saviour: after all, his "interest in her" keeps her "alive". Liberated from one debt, then, she suddenly *owes* Blanco, who thinks he *owns* her:

> His view was that a woman with an ass as skinny as Toby's should consider herself in luck if any man wanted to stick his hole-hammer into her. She'd be even luckier if he didn't sell her to Scales as a temporary, which meant temporarily alive. She should thank her lucky stars. Better, she should thank him: he demanded a thank you after every degrading act. (*Year* 38)

Toby is forced to express gratitude to the self-appointed creditor for "the gift of life" he bestows upon her. Like Scheherazade, who had to keep telling stories to entertain the king, Toby needs to repeat a service to Blanco in order to ward off death. Being "used up soon", however, there seems to be no way out for Toby: "She didn't feel okay, she felt scared. But where else could she go? She lived from pay to pay. She had no money" (*Year* 38, 36). She is trapped, and "[day] by day she was hungrier and more exhausted. She had her own bruises now, like poor Dora's" (*Year* 38).[10] There seems to be no way out for Toby.

However, in a manner true to Atwood, suffering and despair is followed by a return or a rise. It is at the moment when "despair was taking her over" and when "it looked like a dark tunnel" that rescue comes (*Year* 38). Completely fearless, with nothing to lose and a life to save, Adam One—the leader of the eco-religious group, God's Gardeners—shows Toby a way out of despair and captivity. Directed by the Other's need, Adam One challenges the system of domination and exchange that

---

[10] As long as Toby is in need of redemption, she is also bound to victimhood, destined to suffer and unable to act as a redeemer to anyone, including "Poor Dora", whose pain she registers but cannot do anything about.

governs relations in the pleebs. Wrapped in the "humility of swaddling clothes", followed by an army of "raggedly angels", Adam One carries explicit overtones of Christ (*Year* 39). Like Christ bringing hope and light to the fallen, Adam One comes to Toby's rescue and liberates her from bondage. Toby is thus protected from the exploitative and rapacious "agent of extinction", Blanco, and brought into a "crowd of children", who "formed themselves into an honour guard" against Blanco's violent attempts to take his property back (*Year* 42).

Nobody in this dehumanising system can save Toby—help must come from outside the system by someone who does not participate in and perpetuate the exchange mentality. Adam One does not give anything to her owner, Blanco, in exchange for "his worker"; he just shows Toby that there is another way: "Join us, my dear—we are your friends, we have a place for you" (*Year* 41). The image of hands—symbols of our ability to both murder and create—recurs throughout this scene: Blanco's abusive hands, which are placed firmly "on her waist" (*Year* 40) and signal his ownership of Toby, are contrasted with the rescuers', who are, in a gesture of obligation and responsibility, "holding out their hands in greeting" (*Year* 42).

The system, which relies on the disposability of women (and men), may appear intact: somebody else will probably take Toby's place the way she assumed Dora's place once Dora was "used up" and killed off, but the rescue upsets the power balance between master and slave. Toby may be replaceable as an object towards whom Blanco can direct his sexual and violent impulses, but Toby's payback kick (*Year* 41) creates the need for vengeance in Blanco:

> Although he was groggy, his eyes were open and they were fixed on Toby. He'd felt that kick; worse, he'd been humiliated by her in public. He'd lost face. (*Year* 42)

The only one who can free Blanco from the impulse of vengeance is Toby. So, whereas Toby becomes free from Blanco—she does not "need him" for her survival any more—Blanco becomes tied to Toby and thus also to a self-destructive pattern. Anybody can release Blanco from sexual and violent impulses, but only Toby can liberate him from the feelings of shame caused by that kick and the vengeance it activates. The radical break from Blanco has thrown him off balance, indicating that a change to the system is possible.

But, more importantly, the (internal) situation of Toby has changed. This emancipatory moment for Toby—described in terms of "being flooded with the Light of God's Creation" and "a moment she never forgot" (*Year* 43)—not only arrests her fall into death but also shows her another way—an ethical (and spiritual) way. Adam One's rescue thus serves as a catalyst for Toby's inner apocalypse, her inner transformation. The whole rescue scene reminds the reader of a conversion experience: Adam One's intervention has a spiritual, a miraculous, dimension to it and constitutes a significant change in Toby's life: "It was as if a large, benevolent hand had reached down and picked her up, and was holding her safe" (*Year* 43). Acknowledging that the Gardeners "had saved her skin", "she found herself crying with gratitude and relief" (*Year* 47, 43). Gratitude is thus activated in Toby, as is the desire to pay back the gift of a transformed life that is bestowed upon her: "she felt she should pay by working very hard" (*Year* 45-46). This sense of obligation prompts Toby to stay on in the sect and participate in the ethics of care instead of participating in her own and society's destruction. The debt of gratitude that she was forced to express towards Blanco is now redirected towards the Gardeners instead, and consequently she also starts paying back the debt that humanity owes to the planet.

The religious community seizes on the energy—the emotion of gratitude—that is released in Toby, and her capacity for hard work and care is little by little activated. Taken up in a community whose primary goal is the redemption and restoration of God's creation—the planet, humanity, endangered species—the hard work that Toby puts in is for the benefit of the Other. Toby learns how to care for insects and plants, friends as well as strangers. She learns how to save the life of the Other instead of trying to save herself as when she uses "her healing powers to restore Ren"—another female survivor of the Waterless Flood—"coming to see [her] as a 'precious gift'..., as someone to 'cure' and 'cherish'", as Bouson says (22). Together they will then risk their lives to save another female survivor—Amanda, who has been tortured and ruthlessly used and abused by the painballers—emphasising "the feminist ideal of female solidarity" (Bouson 22). Toby also learns to control negative emotions. Her "violent thoughts" about Blanco and her visions of him "stuffed into a garboil boiler, alive" (*Year* 97) are destructive thoughts of revenge, which lead to despair, restless nights and inaction. Pilar, who has registered Toby's pain, her worries about Blanco, directs her to the bees: "You can always tell the bees your troubles" (*Year* 99). As she understands that the bees will react to violent thoughts or actions with a sting, they help Toby let go of negative and destructive thoughts and emotions and instead activate the "endangered" emotions of love and care. Little by little, she learns to cultivate "the higher qualities" of "unselfishness and sharing": Toby "breathed herself in. Her new self" (*Year* 358, 101).

This self-subordination may border on self-effacement, a traditional female role that risks reinforcing victimisation. But Toby's sacrifices make her stronger and more purposeful. In the Pleeblands, Toby was forced into sacrificial behaviour to guarantee her own survival; in the context of the Gardeners, sacrificing her own comforts and life is a free and willing act that takes her towards a new model of coexistence that is not based on exchange or on a master-slave relationship but on charity, the giving of help to those in need with nothing to gain, nothing to profit from it except for the survival of Others and of the planet. By performing God's Gardeners' rituals and rescue operations—by helping those in need, healing those who suffer, forgiving the unforgivable, accepting stewardship of God's garden—Toby repays the gift of life that was bestowed upon her by Adam One and the Gardeners and in the process sees to it that life is passed on to her neighbour and to the planet. It is this obligation towards the Other that inspires hope of redemption not only of the individual but of a planet on the brink of disaster and a humanity on the verge of self-destruction.

Towards a New Plot and an Ethical Function for Art

Through Adam One's rescue, Toby is liberated from victimhood, or at least the kind of victim position that Atwood's heroines often occupy. Like the traditional Atwoodian heroine, Toby falls and rises, but, unlike the traditional Atwoodian heroine, she rises towards assuming ethical responsibility. This pattern is unusual in Atwood's novelistic *oeuvre*. Most of Atwood's female heroines rise after a period of descent and intense suffering, but, contrary to Toby, they seldom rise to redeem the Other. Fully preoccupied with trying to liberate themselves from suffering, they are unable to alleviate or see the suffering of the Other. There is the nameless protagonist in *Surfacing*, who registers Anna's suffering at the hands of her boyfriend, David, but whose concern with her own feelings of guilt incapacitates her to the point where she is unable to intervene on her behalf. There is Elizabeth in *Life Before Man*, who is not free to play a role in the redemption of other women, such as her suicidal sister, because her yearning to save herself is stronger. Too late, she realises that as she "has been concentrating all her energy, for years now, on saving herself. She hasn't had any left over for saving Caroline" (181). There is Elaine in *Cat's Eye*, whose urge to free herself from feelings of shame and guilt makes her blind to Cordelia's as well as other people's suffering.[11] The

---

[11] See Lindhé.

urge to reach beyond an oppressive situation—even though they may themselves perpetuate the disabling emotions that tie them to such a position—keeps them from reaching out to the Other.

The traditional Atwoodian heroine does return or rise after a period of suffering, but the kind of insight or knowledge that the descent (or period of suffering) grants her brings redemption or reconciliation primarily to her. At the end of her life, Elaine realises that the redemptive power that she once identified as otherworldly in the ravine is *within herself*. In a gesture of charity, with hands visible and arms outstretched towards Cordelia, Elaine finally manages to imitate or become the "Virgin Mary" to her childhood "friend", to become a redeemer.[12] But Elaine's transformation comes too late, not for herself but for Cordelia, who is already gone, probably dead. The same holds for Rennie in *Bodily Harm* (1981), who is finally able to touch and reach out to her fellow prisoner, Lora, but by then it is too late. Her touch will in all likelihood not bring Lora—who is beaten beyond the point of recognition—back to life.[13] Only Rennie is rescued. Toby's radical break from victimhood and towards an ethical existence is Atwood's break with a certain kind of plot of suffering and self-redemption, a familiar story or pattern that has held many of Atwood's female protagonists back from addressing themselves to ethical activities such as charity, compassion and forgiveness.[14] The transformation that Toby goes through, however, cannot happen without another individual ready to assume responsibility for the Other, and it cannot happen without religious community.

The Year of the Flood thus marks a new direction in her writing by mapping a religious-ethical way forward. The presence of a religious community, whose focus is on the redemption of the Other, allows Atwood to place her female heroine in a plot pattern that enables Toby to perform ethical activities. Toby is taken up in a context in which Adam One's redemptive mission is enacted—and his words remembered—for

---

[12] The comforting words that Elaine offers to Cordelia at the end of the novel are the same words that were spoken by the Virgin Mary to Elaine herself: "*It's all right. You can go home now*" (419). For a further discussion, see Lindhé.

[13] See Atwood, *Bodily Harm* (particularly 286 and 299).

[14] Amelia Defalco investigates the ethics of care in Atwood's short story collection *Moral Disorder*. She argues that "the need for care dominates these stories: the narrator or protagonist cares for a variety of family members, friends, strangers and even animals. But in these stories the demands of care are never quite met, and none of the characters thrive as a result of the care they receive". Defalco thus suggests that the collection "draws attention to the losses and harm that can come with obligation" (237).

the sake of saving and salvaging the Other. Even after the community is dissolved and many of its members dead, Toby remembers the words of Adam One and acts according to the beliefs established by the community.

Such a community—which provides a basis for ethics—is exactly what is missing in Atwood's *oeuvre*. There is no community available to Elaine that enacts the redemptive mission of her rescuer—the liberating agent that Elaine thinks is the Virgin Mary—or seizes on the powerful emotions that are activated by the rescue.[15] An ethical community is also what seems to be missing in *Life Before Man*, a novel that, according to Theodore Scheckels, is about "a group of people who do not care deeply" (55). The very first sentence of this novel captures the lack of ethical guidelines: "I don't know how I should live" (*Life* 11). With no community that provides a sense of direction or answer to the fundamental ethical question of "how to live"—the characters do not care because they have "practiced not caring" (*Life* 279). Still, the characters long for other-oriented emotions, like Lesje, who is not looking for forgiveness but "would prefer instead to forgive, someone, somehow, for something; but she isn't sure where to begin" (*Life* 311). God's Gardeners offers a fresh start for Toby. The practice of caring emotions, such as compassion, gratitude, healing, forgiveness, love, has a central place in the community of God's Gardeners, thus providing Toby with ethical guidelines of how she should live her life, as well as providing Atwood with a new plot pattern in which her heroine can finally reach out, touch and redeem or save the Other. As the "[external and . . . internal causes of victimisation have been removed", Toby moves into Victim Position Four—the "creative non-victim position" that Atwood outlines in her book *Survival* (38). The game of Victor/Victim belongs to the past, and the energies that were once used to reject or play the role of victim in Blanco's game are channelled into an ethics of care.

Bouson is right when she points out that Atwood "looks to religion—specifically eco-religion—as she seeks evidence of our ethical capacity to find a remedy to humanity's ills" (17).[16] For God's Gardeners, all life is sacred. They recycle everything, and they salvage everything from endangered species to endangered emotions in order to live a sustainable life. They thus offer, as Canavan puts it, "the possibility of an alternative" to the closed capitalistic system (154). But more importantly, this religious community serves as a counterweight to the human urge for (self)redemption.

---

[15] These powerful emotions are instead partly transformed into vengeful behaviour towards Cordelia and partly channelled into her paintings.

[16] For an interesting discussion of God's Gardeners, see Bergthraller.

The religious sect does not encourage its members to have faith in transcendence,[17] but in the redemption of God's creation through the *practice* of care. As Adam One says: "In some religions faith precedes action...In ours, action precedes faith" (*Year* 168).

This is also where the religious sect differs from the other belief system in the trilogy: science. God may be dead to science, but the idea of transcendence is still alive. Crake's paradice project may be an extreme expression of the scientific "ethos", but it nevertheless epitomises what drives science forward: the desire for transcendence. Science, like many religions, accommodates the human desire to be *saved from* something, *to* something, something better beyond our present: whether it is a secular utopian existence—Crake's paradice project—or the latest technology in anti-aging skin care. It is this impulse towards saving oneself—or the belief in salvation—that takes humanity further and further away from ethical responsibility towards the Other. And it is this impulse that God's Gardeners halts by directing its members' attention towards the Other. God's Gardeners also strive for a better beyond, but the path to get there is not through faith or technology but through the practice of care.

As is well known, Atwood "believes in the transformative—and ethical—potential of imaginative literature" (Bouson 23). With the *MaddAddam* trilogy, Atwood attempts to activate readers' concern for the planet. This is precisely where Atwood's insistence that she writes speculative fiction and not science fiction—which, according to Atwood, is not of "this here-and-now Earth"—becomes interesting.[18] Speculative fiction, she argues, goes back to

> Jules Verne's books about submarines and balloon travel and such—things that really could happen but just hadn't completely happened when the authors wrote the books (*Worlds* 6),

and is thus not about "outer space or space invasions" (Atwood "Progressive"). Her speculative fictions, she adamantly claims, contain "no Martians" and are consequently not science fiction (*Worlds* 6). Atwood's rejection of the science fiction label has nothing to do with

---

[17] At the very end of the last book of the trilogy, Toby makes the ultimate sacrifice as she "repay[s] the gift of Life by regifting [herself] to Life", i.e. passing into death. It is in the willingness "to offer ourselves to the great chain of nourishment in our turn" that "the deep meaning of sacrifice" lies, according to Adam One (161, 125).

[18] Atwood suggests that one of the "salient features of SF" is that they are not of "this here-and-now Earth"; see *In Other Worlds* (1).

snobbery or elitism but may rather be a rejection of the possible effects of any otherworldly or extra-terrestrial elements: they may invite readers to imagine a possible other world—or turn their attention beyond "this here-and-now Earth"—and thus cultivate the faith in a way out,[19] which would take humanity away from—not towards—responsibility for the planet. If faith enters into Atwood's speculative fiction, it is faith in the divine within, because this may be the only power left that can help us avoid apocalypse. The only way out seems thus to be within.

Towards Ustopia

In the wake of an inner apocalypse, a woman rises whose rescue by another restores the emotions that the system represses: gratitude, charity, compassion, forgiveness. The redemptive encounter between Adam One and Toby provides the utopic *vision* of—and hope for—a new system in which the basic structuring principle is the redemption of the Other and not of self. Toby's transformation (from victim to redeemer) carries within it the seed of a shift where the current system is replaced by a more Christian-based ethics of charity and stewardship. Such a transformation is not possible without community, and, in *The Year of the Flood*, this community is religious. In Margaret Atwood's imagination, then, religion—one in which the *practice* of care comes before faith (in transcendence and salvation)—plays a key role in transforming the current system. Such a transformation of society—which begins with the individual but cannot come about without (eco-religious) community—seems to me to be Atwood's answer not only to a system that imprisons humans in slavery but also the answer to the present ecological crisis. Atwood has had her vision. Now she leaves us with the following question: are we willing to pay the ultimate price—the price of human apocalypse for the sake of instant gratifications—or are we, like Toby, ready to start paying back now and thus move towards a more hopeful future—towards ustopia—in which we are still *in* the story?

---

[19] The science fiction genre is often said to accommodate the impulse for—or belief in—transcendence; see, for example, Cowan.

Works Cited

Atwood, Margaret. *Bodily Harm*. 1981. Reprint. New York: Bantam Books, 1982. Print.

—. *Cat's Eye*. 1988. London: Virago, 2002. Print.

—. *In Other Worlds: SF and the Human Imagination*. New York: Anchor Books, 2011. Print.

—. *Life Before Man*. 1979. Reprint. London: Virago Press, 1982. Print.

—. "A Progressive Interview with Margaret Atwood". Interview by Matthew Rothschild. The *Progressive Magazine*. 2 Dec. 2010. Web. 13 May 2014.

—. *Surfacing*. 1972. Reprint. New York: Doubleday, 1998. Print.

—. *Survival: A Thematic Guide to Canadian Literature*. Toronto: Anansi, 1972. Print.

—. *The Year of the Flood*. New York: Doubleday, 2009. Print.

Bergthraller, Hannes. "Housebreaking the Human Animal: Humanism and the Problem of Sustainability in Margaret Atwood's *Oryx and Crake* and *The Year of the Flood*". *English Studies* 91.7 (2010): 728-743. Print.

Bouson, Brooks J. "'We're Using up the Earth. It's Almost Gone': A Return to the Post-Apocalyptic Future in Margaret Atwood's *The Year of the Flood*". *The Journal of Commonwealth Literature* 46.1 (2011): 9-26. Print.

Canavan, Gerry. "Hope, But Not for Us: Ecological Science Fiction and the End of the World in Margaret Atwood's *Oryx and Crake* and *The Year of the Flood*". *LIT: Literature Interpretation Theory* 23.2 (2012): 138-159. Print.

Cowan, Douglas E. *Sacred Space: The Quest for Transcendence in Science Fiction and Television*. Waco: Baylor UP, 2010. Print.

Croteau, Melissa. "Introduction". *Apocalyptic Shakespeare: Essays on Visions of Chaos and Revelation in Recent Film Adaptations*. Eds. Melissa Croteau and Carolyn Jess-Cooke. Jefferson: McFarland & Company, 2009: 1-28. Print.

Defalco, Amelia. "Moral Obligation, Disordered Care: The Ethics of Caregiving in Margaret Atwood's *Moral Disorder*". *Contemporary Literature* 52.2 (2011): 236-263. Print.

Fitting, Peter. "Utopia, Dystopia and Science Fiction". *The Cambridge Companion to Utopian Literature*. Ed. Gregory Claeys. Cambridge: Cambridge UP, 2010: 135-153. Print.

Jameson, Frederic. *Archeologies of the Future: The Desire Called Utopia and Other Science Fictions*. London: Verso, 2005. Print.

Knickerbocker, Dale. "Apocalypse, Utopia, and Dystopia: Old Paradigms Meet a New Millennium". *Extrapolation* 51.3 (2010): 345-357. Print.

Lindhé, Anna. "Sisterhood, Shame, and Redemption in *Cat's Eye* and *King Lear*". *Margaret Atwood Studies* 7 (2013): 11-24. Print.

Mohr, Dunja M. "Transgressive Utopian Dystopias: The Postmodern Reappearance of Utopia in the Disguise of Dystopia". *ZAA* 55.1 (2007): 5-24. Print.

Scheckels, Theodore F. *The Political in Margaret Atwood's Fiction: The Writing on the Wall of the Tent.* Farnham: Ashgate, 2012. Print.

Tolan, Fiona. *Margaret Atwood: Feminism and Fiction.* Amsterdam: Rodopi, 2007. Print.

Woolf, Virginia. *To the Lighthouse.* 1927. Reprint. Hertfordshire: Wordsworth Editions Limited: 1994. Print.

CHAPTER FIVE

WRITING FROM THE MARGIN: VICTIM POSITIONS IN ATWOOD'S *THE YEAR OF THE FLOOD*

MILES WEAFER

Introduction

In *The Year of the Flood*, the second instalment of her dystopic *MaddAddam* trilogy, Margaret Atwood reveals her post-apocalyptic world from its margins. In contrast to the trilogy's first instalment, *Oryx and Crake*, whose protagonist "Snowman"/Jimmy recalls his life alongside star pupil-turned mad scientist "Crake"/Glenn inside the elite, walled corporate research compounds and academic institutions, *The Year of the Flood* concerns itself with women who inhabit the failed suburbs, slums, religious cult compounds and strip clubs comprising the outlying "pleebland" ghettos. *Flood*'s readers are aligned with Toby and Ren: women who survive the "Waterless Flood" plague designed by Crake/Glenn, while hermetically sealed in an abandoned beauty salon and an abandoned strip club, respectively, and reliant on the training obtained during their tenure in the marginalised doomsday eco-Christian cult, the God's Gardeners.

The ecological themes of Atwood's series have been popularly acknowledged—perhaps most notably by environmentalist and humanitarian Stephen Lewis alongside *Flood*'s entry into Canada's national "battle of the books" in 2013 ("Here and Now Toronto"). Yet *The Year of the Flood* and the *MaddAddam* series as a whole are also notably stories of survival—a theme familiar to, and characteristic of, an author whose earliest publications include the 1972 thematic guide to Canadian literature, *Survival*; Atwood identifies survival as the central symbol for Canadian authors who, grounded in the realities of an unforgiving landscape and a history of colonial exploitation, confront nature not as a sublime or contemplative place but, rather, as hostile elements to be survived (32). Enmeshed in the intertwined themes of a hostile environment and survival as they arise in Canadian literature, Atwood develops a model of four Victim Positions that provide a strategy for addressing and for overcoming victimhood for marginalised individuals, groups and nations. In short, these Victim Positions are: 1) denial of victimhood; 2) acknowledgement of victimhood and displacement of its source; 3) acknowledgement of the source of victimhood and confronting victimhood as inescapable and; 4) overcoming victimhood by becoming what she calls a "creative non-victim" (*Survival* 36-39).

This chapter applies the Victim Positions outlined by Atwood to four female protagonists occupying the dystopian world of the *MaddAddam* series—three of whom are central to its second instalment, *The Year of the Flood*. Drawing on my training in Canadian communication scholarship, and as a way to emphasise the theme of marginality, which, in the mode of colonialism, frames survival and victimhood as specifically Canadian themes for Atwood, I will place Atwood's theses on survival in dialogue with the role of the "margin" addressed by Harold Innis and his commentators. For Innis and his commentators, "the margin", understood as a space

> drawn into the axes of imperial economy, administration, and information but which remains "behind" (to put it in temporal terms) or "outside" (spatially speaking) in terms of economic and political power (Berland 77),

operates as the chief force of critical insight and historical change; while the places and institutions central to dominant systems of exchange and communication enjoy a privileged place in the dissemination of ideas and a legitimation of explanation over our world—a situation Innis terms a "monopoly of knowledge"—outlying, marginalised places, groups and communicative or cultural practices provide the critical insight that can balance and correct the alienating impact of dominant empires, communicative practices and cultural logics. Complementing the literary analysis provided by Atwood's victim positions, the concept of the margin, as it appears in Innisian scholarship, allows one to align the various characters, positions and journeys in Atwood's dystopian world with their victimisation by, and potential subversion of, the story's dominant, and ultimately repressive, institutions.

In what follows, I will first detail the concept of the "margin" as it appears in Innisian scholarship before aligning four characters in the *MaddAddam* series with Atwood's four Victim Positions. I will then relate Atwood's formulation of survival with Innis's formulation of the margin, aligning Atwood's "creative non-victim" with Innis's formulation of subversive, marginal cultural production. Finally, I will frame Atwood's own writing as critical practice aligned with her own marginality as a Canadian writer.

Harold Innis and the subversive power of the margin

Economic historian and communication scholar Harold Innis (1894-1952) was perhaps Canada's first internationally known scholar. University of Toronto's Innis College, located near Atwood's "Annex" neighbourhood, bears his name. Innis's most important contribution to communication studies is his characterisation of contemporary, western civilisation as "space-biased", or dominated by media and institutions that favour spatial extension over temporal endurance. Innis's account of history traces the growth and decay of various institutionalisations of power—or *empires*—according to their dominant avenues of trade, transportation and communication: a materialist methodology derived from his economic histories of Canada's various successive raw material exports, or "staples".[1] He detailed how the institutionalised, geographically articulated process of extensive resource collection, centralised industrial refinement or assemblage and wide re-distribution of manufactured commodities creates a relative, unequal relationship of dependency between the outlying resource-offering regions and countries, and the production centres at the heart of national and colonial empires. Innis identified how power and knowledge take shape according to a centralising, spatial dynamic; monopolistic ownership or control over resource extraction, commodity production and transportation is paralleled by dominant institutional control over knowledge production and transmission, whereby a few dominant institutions enjoy a legitimacy of explanation and control of our world. Innis's stress on the centralising effect of contemporary Western institutions also emphasises the margins of empire.

While marginal regions, communities and cultural practices are relatively excluded from dominant forms of industry, cultural and knowledge production, and political power, they are not outside of empire, nor are they absent from history; rather, the margin, in Innis's formulation, remains the most significant source of critical insight and historical change. Judith Stamps equates Innis's formulation of the margin with the counter-thesis of the dialectic; marginalised knowledge and cultural

---

[1] See, for instance, *A History of the Canadian Pacific Railway* (1923), *The Fur Trade in Canada* (1930) and *The Cod Fisheries: The History of an International Economy* (1940).

production function as empire's negation, as an "essential (source) or critique" whose problematic relation with dominant imperial centres and transmission practices reveal the contradictions and inconsistencies of the world and our knowledge of it (46). For Innis, a monopoly or oligopoly of knowledge is built up to the point that equilibrium is disturbed *at its margins*, where "creative, expressive use of small format media could offset the alienating impact of mass media" (Salter 193).

The religious and cultural practice of the God's Gardeners (led by the mysterious priest, "Adam One") functions as an ecologically-based critique of the bioengineering and short-sighted instrumental logic central to *Flood*'s corporate compounds, and as a resistance to the imperial rule effected by their secret police, the CorpSeCorps:

> The Compounds were where the Corps people lived—all those scientists and business people Adam One said were destroying old Species and making new ones and ruining the world... (Atwood *Flood* 146)

The Gardeners view human beings' own capacity for information storage and transmission as sacred and redemptive:

> A massive die-off of the human race was impending, due to overpopulation and wickedness, but the Gardeners exempted themselves: they intended to float above the Waterless Flood...As for the flotation devices in which they would ride out this flood, they themselves would be their own Arks, stored with their own collections of inner animals, or at least the names of those animals. Thus they would survive to replenish the Earth. (47)

As for the Gardeners' environmental practices—which go beyond recycling and vegetarianism to pedantic practices such as "slug relocation"—their most effective preparation for their own cultural survival as outlaws in a police state, and their own bare survival after the apocalyptic Waterless Flood, involves prioritising the kind of participatory oral cultural practice that Innis would call "time-biased". Rhyming mnemonic devices, including Gardener hymns inspired in part by the Anglican and United Churches of Canada (433)—transmit culture without the written residue that enables detection; writing, Ren recalls, was dangerous because "your enemies could trace you through it, and hunt you down, and use your words to condemn you" (6). Likewise, human memory, trained by participatory intergenerational transmission, endures in ways that space-biased writing technology—including print media and datasets—cannot:

> This is what the Gardeners taught us, when I was a child among them. They told us to depend on memory because nothing written down could be relied on. The Spirit travels from mouth to mouth, not from thing to thing: books could be burnt, paper crumble away, computers could be destroyed. (6)

Just as Innis identifies temporally enduring communicative and cultural practice as the saviour of our spatially masterful, but short-sighted, Western world, so do Atwood's Gardeners depend on it for their survival as individuals, as a culture and as a species. While Atwood classifies the Victim Positions facing individuals, groups and nations (including herself, and her own) marginalised by today's systemic power structures—most notably patriarchy, colonialism and capitalism—the *MaddAddam* series, and *Flood* in particular, marks a continued effort to explore the narrative and critical possibilities offered by her decades-old critical-literary model.

Atwood's Survival and the Movement towards Creative Non Victimhood

Atwood uses Canada's tough natural environment and colonial status as starting points for linking nature to survival and for developing Victim Positions, including her strategy of "creative non victimhood", out of Canadian literature. While this project started four decades ago in her thematic guide to Canadian literature, the framework outlined and applied in *Survival* continues to guide her own writing, including (and perhaps especially) the *MaddAddam* series. While animals have a special place in Canadian literature, including Atwood's significant contributions (Canadians often write from the animal's point of view, she argues, often as the animal fights for its own survival) (*Survival* 74), it is important to stress that for Atwood's literary victims—those she encounters and those she creates—the harsh, victimising natural environment often serves as a means of dressing up the systemic power relations that victimise protagonists, whether they, or their readers, recognise it or not. As Atwood puts it:

> But you might wonder, in a snowstorm-kills-man story, whether the snowstorm is an adequate explanation for the misery of the character, or whether the author has displaced the source of the misery in their world and is blaming the snowstorm when they ought to be blaming something else. (*Survival* 41)

The Year of The Flood, however, operates as speculative fiction to explicitly align natural disaster with a hyper-capitalist world and scientific industrial complex extrapolated from our own world. Protagonists survive the environmental apocalypse only after surviving a dystopic world that is all too familiar for many of us today.

The systemic power relations encountered by *Flood*'s female protagonists undoubtedly belong to capitalism and patriarchy, and can be identified with the elite individuals—mostly men—occupying the bioengineering compounds and universities in which *Oryx and Crake* is set. The women central to both books provide snapshots of individuals occupying the four Victim Positions detailed by Atwood in 1972.

"Oryx", the love object of both Snowman/Jimmy—*Oryx and Crake*'s protagonist—and Crake/Glenn—the engineer of the apocalyptic "Waterless Flood"—denies her victimhood. Oryx recounts her childhood as a beggar and child pornography participant amidst abject poverty in what seems to be the so-called "developing world": an upbringing so far in the margins it is virtually unimaginable for anyone in the book and, presumably, for most of its readers. Yet Oryx continually sympathises with her traffickers and captors. The golden-wristwatched "Uncle En", who purchased her from her village as a child, gave the remaining children "a better chance in life" (*Oryx* 117); his recognition of the children's monetary value gave them something more "dependable" than love (126); "he could have done much worse things to [her], and he didn't do them"; hence he wasn't all about money, and he liked her (136). Jack, the child pornographer, never had her do anything lovers do not; besides, he taught her to speak and read English (141). Oryx's apparent captors in the western world, who kept her locked in their garage, were trying to be helpful (316)**.** As an adult sex worker, Oryx is purchased by Crake/Glenn (via student services), and he later puts her to work training his posthuman race, securely locked in his privately funded geodesic dome-enclosed artificial garden ("The Paradice Project"); Oryx sees this labour as honourable work for a genius boss, despite his hand constantly "on her shoulder, her arm, her small waist, perfect butt"— a hand that, according to the (admittedly scorned) Jimmy, says, *"Mine, mine"* (313). Finally, when Crake/Glenn uses Oryx to distribute his sterilisation drug (which she may or may not know is also a deadly plague), disguised as a sex drug, contraceptive and immunity potion, Oryx defends this too, arguing that Crake simply recognises the dangers of, and solution to, overpopulation ("There are too many people and *that* makes the people bad. Crake is a very smart man!" [322, emphasis added]). Oryx herself never escapes her captivity in the inner dome of the Paradice

Project, eventually having her throat slit by her lover/captor/boss once his plan is set in motion (329).

Oryx's attitude corresponds to Victim Position One: to deny the fact of victimhood. Subjects in Position One "spend time explaining away the obvious" and "pretending that certain visible facts do not exist" (Atwood *Survival* 36). Oryx, congruent with victims in Position One, is better off than others in her group, and likely afraid to recognise victimhood for fear of losing her acquired privilege. This is not surprising for one originating so far in the margins yet occupying a place so close to the centre of power.

Ren, the young protagonist of *Flood*, seems to identify her own victimhood, or at realise she is in danger. Yet, characteristic of Atwood's second Victim Position, Ren overlooks the powerful, destructive or oppressive roles of many closest to her. Having grown up in the HealthWyzer compound, Ren is taken by her mother to live with the Gardeners at age ten amidst a whirlwind romance/strategic relationship with one of its key agents.[2] Yet Ren and her mother return to the HealthWyzer compound by the time she's in high school (where she has her heart broken by Jimmy). Ren soon flees her life in the compound to work at the elite, animal-themed sex club, Scales and Tails; there she survives the plague in the airlocked "sticky zone", quarantined after having her bird-themed "Biofilm Bodysuit" ruptured by an overzealous client. Ren is eventually rescued by her friend Amanda, reunited with childhood friends, raped by thugs and left for dead, nursed to life by former Gardener matriarch Toby. By the end of *Flood*, Ren accompanies Toby on a risky mission to rescue Amanda from her violent outlaw captors.

Atwood describes the second Victim Position as acknowledgment of victimhood but misidentification of its source (*Survival* 37). This confused position best describes Ren. She acknowledges her *vulnerability* on multiple occasions; during her high school years at the compound, Ren admits she's "sad underneath" (*Flood* 218), and, later, as the plague erupts outside, Ren acknowledges the cell-like nature of the "sticky zone" if not the entrapping qualities of the sex-club where she worked (283). Upon encountering Oryx at Scales, Ren shows more insight than Oryx herself, acknowledging that they are both "girls for rent" (306). Ren doesn't espouse that victimhood is avoidable—a quality characteristic of the more privileged victims Atwood situates in Position One; in contrast, Ren often promotes her own selflessness, emphasising the victimisation of others to

---

[2] The agent being Zeb, the key protagonist of Atwood's third installment, *MaddAddam*, whose story goes beyond the scope of this paper.

avoid addressing her own (when she and Amanda are captured and raped, she denies thinking about it, arguing that "[it] was worse for Amanda than for me" [342]). Yet Ren denies the role of the men closest to her in the capitalist and patriarchal system in which she is trapped. She denies that her real father in the HealthWyzer compound contributes to the destruction of old Species and dangerous creation of new ones (146). Likewise, Ren defends her bouncer/pimp as a man of ethics because, while he pats her on the bum, he never took freebies; Ren sees him as the closest thing to a father she would get (303). While Ren rarely, if ever, expresses anger, her defining emotions are fear and confused helplessness. Characteristic of a victim in Position Two, Ren sees here employment as a sex worker as an act of Fate and refuses to decide how much of her situation is unchangeable: "Everything was ruined and destroyed", Ren claims, "and there was no safe place for me" (302).

Toby is the other key protagonist of *Flood*, though she does not share Ren's first person narrative role. A generation older than Ren, Toby also has a rougher past than Ren and expresses a more proactive attitude towards the systemic oppression and violence they endure and the plague they survive. Toby is born in blue-collar suburbs in conditions less marginalised than Oryx's abject poverty (a "tacky little split-level" [20] in an older Pleeb), though beyond the walls of Ren's native HealthWyzer compound. Toby is orphaned amidst a hypercapitalist system, her mother the victim of a destructive pharmaceutical-industrial complex and her father a victim of bankruptcy and, eventually, suicide; Toby makes it on her own by selling her hair and ova (32), and eventually working in the mystery meat fast-food industry where she is violently raped by her mob-tied manager. Eventually rescued by the Gardeners, Toby becomes a powerful matriarch in their ranks and falls in love with the agent serving, for a time, as Ren's stepfather.

Toby is a survivor in the most profound, noble and active sense of the word. Active and focused at the time of the Waterless Flood, Toby secures herself in an elite spa where the Gardeners found her refuge. She eventually returns to her suburb amidst the destruction, refusing to resemble prey (22) and recovering the rifle her late father buried in her childhood yard (20). Epitomising a victim occupying Atwood's Third Position, Toby acknowledges her victimhood as a fact but, for a time at least, refuses "to accept the assumption that the role is inevitable";[3] she identifies and directs her anger at the personification of her oppressor

---

[3] "Position Three: *To acknowledge the fact that you are a victim but to refuse to accept the assumption that the role is inevitable*" (Atwood *Survival* 37).

Blanco—the outlaw manager who raped her, Ren and Amanda—and channels her anger into constructive action: she kills Blanco with opiates and poisonous mushrooms. Ren looks up to Toby; while the Gardener children see her as hard and emotionless, giving her the name "The Dry Witch", Ren states that you need something dry to hold on to when you feel you're sinking.

However, reflecting Atwood's insistence that the Positions are fluid ("you're rarely in any Position in its pure form for very long" [*Survival* 39]), Toby struggles with the objective fact of her victimhood and her power to move beyond it. Initially seeing the impending ecological disaster as means to give up one's agency ("You find yourself saying to the sky, *Just do it. Do your worst. Get it over with*" [239]), Toby later rejects feeling sorry for herself in favour of progressive action; "It's wrong", she thinks "to give so much time over to mourning...Mourning and brooding. There's nothing to be accomplished by it" (96). In Position Three, Atwood stresses,

> You can make real decisions about how much of your position can be changed and how much can't (you can't make it stop snowing, you can stop blaming the snow for everything that's wrong). (*Survival* 38)

Ultimately, however, Toby stakes her happiness on Zeb. When he does not return from a battle in Atwood's third instalment, *MaddAddam*, Toby becomes locked into her sadness, to use Atwood's phrase (*Survival* 38), and finds herself back in Position Two: seemingly inevitable victimhood.[4] In the end, Toby kills herself with the same opiates she used to subdue her tormentor; just as nature intoxicates as it immobilises ("The sound is lulling. Stay here. Sink down. Go to sleep" [327]), so too, it seems, does victimhood.

One of the most important characters of *Flood* is Amanda Payne; while arguably marginal to the narrative, Amanda personifies the focal point of both Atwood's critical-theoretical project in *Survival* and Atwood's own creative-progressive objectives as a writer. Aside from Oryx, Amanda originates from the most marginal place of all characters in the series. Similar to Toby, Amanda is orphaned by financial disaster coupled with deteriorating parental health (84). Amanda flees a disease-ridden refugee camp in Texas and burrows her way under the (familiar, but more

---

[4] Position Two "is a dynamic position, rather than a static one; from it you can move on to Position Four, but if you become locked into your anger and fail to change your situation, you might well find yourself back in Position Two" (*Survival* 38).

northern) wall designed to keep Tex-Mex refugees out (95) changing her name from the "white-trash name", Barb Jones, in the process (85). Part of a "Pleebrat" gang in one of the seedier ghettos surrounding the Gardeners' compound, Amanda is befriended by Ren and taken in to her blended family. Amanda grows up to be an artist, securing corporate grants and keeping in touch with Ren throughout Ren's teenage and young adult years. Having resourcefully survived the chaos of the Flood to free Ren from her quarantine, Amanda is eventually captured by a gang of murderous outlaws affiliated with Toby's late tormentor.

Toby is inspired by Amanda ("Even Dry Witch Toby would brighten up when she saw Amanda coming" [83]), as is Ren, who, reflecting on Amanda's journey from Texas, states,

> In her place I would have just laid down in a ditch and cried myself to death. But Amanda says if there's something you really want, you can figure out a way to get it. (85)

Though Amanda finds herself in dire peril by the end of *Flood*, Amanda's activity throughout the novel defines her role. Amanda epitomises the creative non-victim, occupying "Position Four" in Atwood's framework: one who is able to accept his/her own experience "for what it is, rather than having to distort it to make it correspond with others' versions", especially those of their oppressors (*Survival* 39). For Amanda, energy is no longer suppressed, displaced or used for "dynamic anger" (Atwood *Survival* 38); rather, it is used for creative, artistic practice. From her childhood, Amanda is a writer of sorts, as witnessed by Ren when they first meet:

> She'd written her name in syrup on (a concrete slab) and a stream of ants was feeding on the letters, to that each letter had an edging of black ants. That was how I first learned Amanda's name—I saw it written in ants. Amanda Payne. (*Flood* 86)

Ren admires the invisibility Amanda acquired by changing her name from Barb Jones (85), and Amanda's early artistic practice reflects Amanda's control over her own image and experience. It is also congruent with the Gardeners' wariness of the written word:

> "It's neat," said Amanda. "You write things, then they eat your writing. So you appear, then you disappear. That way no one can find you." (86)

Amanda's practice is intensified in her corporate-sponsored "Bioart installations"—one being cow bones caked in syrup, eventually covered in insects, and videotaped from a bird's-eye view. Amanda "liked to watch things move and grow and disappear" (56).

Aside from Atwood's description of the creative non-victim, Amanda's art practice is best contextualised according the mythology Snowman/Jimmy creates for Crake/Glenn's posthuman people, the "Crakers". Whereas Crake created the Crakers, the animals "hatched out of an egg, a giant egg laid by Oryx herself" (*Oryx* 96). "Actually", Snowman says, "she laid two eggs":

> one full of animals and birds and fish, and the other one full of words. But the egg full of words hatched first, and the (people) had already been created by then, and they'd eaten up all the words because they were hungry, and so there were no words left over when the second egg hatched out. And that is why the animals can't talk. (96)

Amanda's art practice literally gives words to hungry animals.

Conclusion: Giving Words to Animals

Like Amanda's art, survival-oriented Canadian literature also gives words to animals, albeit in a more figurative sense. Atwood proposes that while English animal stories are about "social relations", and American animal stories about people killing animals, Canadian animal stories "are about *being* killed, as felt emotionally from inside the fur and feathers" (*Survival* 74). Atwood's literary contributions are no exception; *Flood*'s victims conceal themselves in the artificial skins of animals, whether it be Oryx "dressed" in an animal's name, Ren in the bird-themed Biofilm Bodysuit she acquires at Scales and Tails, or Toby, who, for a time, works as a promotional "furzooter", "dressing up as bears and tigers and lions and other endangered species she could hear being slaughtered on the floor below her" (31). Yet Amanda's creative practice must be closest to Atwood's heart, as a writer. Writers "*by definition*", Atwood argues, are in "Position Four at the moment of writing, that is, the moment of creation" (*Survival* 40). And whether it's bioart installation work, like Amanda's, or novel-writing, like Atwood's, art is what is left over "[when] any civilization is dust and ashes…Imaginative structures. Meaning—human meaning—is defined by them" (*Oryx* 167). In terms of critical, subversive power, art is a major thorn in the side of Crake/Glenn (*"As soon as they start doing art, we're in trouble"* [*Oryx* 361])—whose destructive plan is developed in the central, intertwined space of patriarchy and capitalist industry.

This chapter offers a departure point for applying Atwood's Basic Victim Positions to characters in *Oryx and Crake* and *The Year of the Flood*. While I've focused on protagonists central to *The Year of the Flood*, characters beyond my frame of analysis may fit Atwood's framework (men like "Adam One" and Zeb—the focus of Atwood's third instalment, *MaddAddam*—are excellent examples of creative non-victims). I have focused my analysis on women whose marginality informs their assumption of various Victim Positions. Other readers may find ways to categorise characters that may or may not be congruent with what I have presented above. This is not a problem; Atwood stresses that her own thematic guide is "intended to be suggestive rather than totally accurate" as

> experience is never linear: you're rarely in any Position in its pure form for
> very long—and you may have a foot...in more than one Position at once.
> (*Survival* 39)

Oryx, one could argue, loses her opportunity to move beyond Position One, whereas the challenge for Ren and for Toby is to get to Position Four.

I have also suggested that survival and victimhood, in these two novels, are intertwined with a negotiation of "the margin" as it is formulated by Innis and his commentators; the more marginalised the victim, the better opportunity they have of achieving creative non-victimhood. Additionally, while Innis was never a literary critic, Innis's thoughts on media—specifically his distinctions between written and oral communication and culture—resonate with Atwood's treatment of media and communication in *The Year of the Flood*. Innis's critical theory, which develops out of his attention to avenues of transportation, is also useful in that it treats power as dynamic rather than static; Innisian scholarship traces the circulation of power. Evident in the movement of characters in *Oryx and Crake* and *The Year of the Flood*, power does not rest in the centre of institutions and systems—it circulates from the centre, to the margin and back again; Oryx originates in the furthest of margins, but ends her life in the centre. Ren is born within the walls of the HealthWyzer compound, but she finds herself moving to Pleeblands to live among the Gardeners, only to return to the compound and wind up in the margins again. Toby moves from the suburbs to the slums, from the Gardeners enclave to an elite spa and, eventually, out into the post-apocalyptic natural world itself. Amanda, whose appearance in the story depends on her penetration of a militarised barricade, moves from the roughest of slums to the elite, corporate-sponsored art world, only to return and free

Ren from a padlocked quarantine. Boundaries exist—the compounds themselves may be perceived (by Amanda) as castles or jails (206)—but boundaries are crossed, checkpoints are averted, Biofilm Bodysuits are ripped, information leaks and knowledge, in Ren's words, is "caught…like germs" (67). The Gardeners themselves "use a lot of soap, because they were so worried about microbes" (68), and the same Gardeners' membership contributes to Crake/Glenn's master plan of mass destruction. What matters then, is not where boundaries lie—whether they be boundaries between physical zones, between organisms or between Victim Positions—but, rather, who moves through them and how their movement is motivated, enabled and constrained. As Crake/Glenn tells Toby, the centre of power today "wouldn't be a single person, it would be the technological connections" (229). Crake/Glenn himself is perhaps the most mobile character of all, serving as the intermediary between the most elite and manufactured corridors and the marginalised Gardiners themselves.

The Year of the Flood demonstrates that although the margin is relatively less powerful than the centre, the margin is the key source of critical insight and historical change. Individuals and groups marginalised or colonised by the centre can also inhabit a novel and disruptive point of view like the skin of an animal and use their multiple viewpoints to disrupt the oppressive intertwining of knowledge and industry that Innis would term a "monopoly of knowledge". This kind of subversive energy emerges amidst the creative dialogical use of small format media exemplified by Amanda's bioart installations and Atwood's novels. Plato argues that the written word is problematic because, however many times you read it, it can only give you the same answer.[5] Yet, evident in potential reworkings of Atwood's protagonists and Victim Positions, *Oryx and Crake* and *The Year of the Flood* do not give readers the same answers every time. Atwood carefully notes that *Survival* provides "a skeleton of Canadian literature": "a static dissection" to facilitate classification, "rather than a dynamic examination of a process-in-motion" (40). Art, on the other hand, is engaged with life and movement. Good art wiggles under its readers' gazes, like ants in syrup.

Works Cited

Atwood, Margaret. *Oryx and Crake*. Toronto: Vintage Canada, 2009. Print.

---

[5] See *Phaedrus*, line 275E.

—. *Survival: A Thematic Guide to Canadian Literature*. Toronto: Anansi, 1972. Print.

—. *The Year of the Flood*. Toronto: Vintage Canada, 2010. Print.

Berland, Jody. *North of Empire: Essays on the Cultural Technology of Space*. Durham and London: Duke University Press, 2009. Print.

"Here and Now Toronto". *Canada Reads: Stephen Lewis Defends Margaret Atwood*. Toronto Broadcasting Centre: Canadian Broadcasting Corporation, 27 November 2013. Web. 2 July 2014.

Innis, Harold. *The Bias of Communication*. Toronto: University of Toronto Press, 1951. Print.

—. *The Cod Fisheries: The History of an International Economy*. Toronto: The Ryerson Press, 1940. Print.

—. *Empire and Communications*. Oxford: Clarendon Press, 1950. Print.

—. *The Fur Trade in Canada*. Toronto: University of Toronto Press, 1930. Print.

—. *A History of the Canadian Pacific Railway*. Toronto: University of Toronto Press, 1923. Print.

Plato. *Phaedrus*. Indianapolis/Cambridge: Hackett Publishing Company, 1995. Print.

Salter, Liora. "'Public' and Mass Media in Canada: Dialects in Innis' Communication Analysis". *Culture, Communication, and Dependency: The Tradition of H.A. Innis*. Eds. William H. Melody, Liora Salter and Paul Heyher. Norwood, New Jersey: Ablex, 1981. 193-207. Print.

Stamps, Judith. *Unthinking Modernity: Innis, McLuhan, and the Frankfurt School*. Montreal: McGill Queens University Press, 1995. Print.

CHAPTER SIX

SURVIVAL IN THE POST-APOCALYPSE: ECOFEMINISM IN *MADDADDAM*

ANNA BEDFORD

In her 1972 guide to Canadian literature, Margaret Atwood identified survival as a key theme. The trope she finds central to Canadian literature is imbued with special urgency in an apocalyptic setting. As I look at Atwood's perilous future of destructive capitalist science, the exploitation of nature and the debasement of life, I identify ecofeminist concerns and suggest that ecofeminist ethics and practices are key to surviving the apocalypse—for human and non-human alike. I will begin my analysis by considering how Atwood's trilogy depicts the urgent dangers of capitalism and the instrumental approach to nature, animals and Others. I will then argue that these novels offer an ecofeminist alternative to capitalist exploitation that is located in the teachings of ecofeminist philosophies, ethics of care, connection and communities rather than individual self-preservation.

Oryx and Crake (2003)

The first novel in the trilogy, *Oryx and Crake,* is told from the perspective of "Snowman", who has survived the apocalypse—so far. A great deal of the tale is a retrospective, as Snowman looks back to a society now wiped out, and a time when he was called "Jimmy". Through Snowman's reminiscences, the reader slowly learns how the human population was nearly eradicated by a bioengineered pandemic plague, secretly spread through a sex enhancement drug called BlyssPluss, and how Snowman/Jimmy came to be alone on a beach, possibly the last human alive, with a strange group of genetically modified people who are nicknamed the "Children of Crake" or "Crakers".

The two other central characters, for whom the novel is named, are Oryx and Crake. Both are dead by the time of the narrative. Crake is Jimmy's brilliant childhood best friend, who grew up to become a scientist and to successfully engineer this new species of people. Oryx is a woman Jimmy and Crake saw on a "kiddie porn" internet site when she was a small girl (and they themselves young teens). Later, at college, Crake requests a woman who would match the screenshot of that girl and hires her to work for him. Jimmy falls immediately in love with Oryx, seeming always to believe she is the very same woman who captivated him on the internet when he was an adolescent.

Crake, after perfecting his new race of people, disburses a pandemic plague to wipe out the entire human race, apart from himself, Jimmy, Oryx and the Children, who were in a sealed base called "Paradice". Crake then slits Oryx's throat in front of Jimmy, knowing his friend will be compelled to shoot him as he witnesses the death of the woman he loves so obsessively, and therefore manipulating Jimmy into a kind of assisted suicide. Snowman/Jimmy is now left obligated by his promise to his beloved Oryx to care for the Crakers, and trying, himself, to survive. The novel ends uncertainly, with Snowman battling an infection and his discovery that there are three other humans who have arrived on the beach.

The Year of the Flood (2009)

The Year of the Flood's narrative overlaps in several places with that of *Oryx and Crake*. The story is told from the perspectives of two women, Toby and Ren. They both come, by chance and some reluctance, to join a band of vegetarian ecological activists—the God's Gardeners—living in a counter-culture commune on a reclaimed and repurposed rooftop, the Edencliff Rooftop Garden.

The first narrator we meet is Toby, a young woman who lost her parents due to lack of available medical care, bankruptcy and desperation. Toby ends up working in a fast food burger joint run by a member of the mob, who is also a painballer—a convicted criminal who has fought to the death and been released victorious. Toby is this manager's, Blanco's, latest "girlfriend", already decorated with bruises and beginning to fear for her life when the God's Gardeners parade through the streets. During a confrontation between the Gardeners and Blanco, Toby throws her own kick at Blanco's head and then has to flee with them. She finds a new home on the Edencliff Rooftop and later becomes a female leader, an Eve. Blanco, humiliated and vengeful, eventually tracks Toby down and begins stalking her. The Gardener leaders hide her in a high-end corporate spa,

AnooYoo, which is where she waits out the Waterless Flood (Crake's plague), using Gardener skills to grow food and survive.

The second narrator, whose story is interspersed with Toby's, is Ren. Ren joins the Gardeners as a child when her mother sneaks out of their corporate compound, daughter in tow, to follow a new boyfriend, the Gardener, Zeb. Ren arrives on the Rooftop as an adolescent, when Toby is already an Eve and one of her new teachers. She slowly adjusts and makes a best friend in the worldly Amanda, a street child Ren recruits to live with her among the Gardeners. Ren is then uprooted again when her mother leaves Zeb and returns to the HealthWyzer compound. Amanda and Ren reunite while Amanda is at university, where Ren discovers her friend is dating the same Jimmy who was her high school boyfriend and whom the audience recognises as Snowman, the protagonist of *Oryx and Crake*.

Ren becomes a trapeze artist and dancer at a high-end sex club, Scales and Tails. It's in this setting, locked in a decontamination room after her biofilm ruptured during an exchange, that Ren experiences the Waterless Flood. She survives eating canned food, watching the devastation unfold on the television, while broadcasts last. She waits for Amanda to arrive to unlock the door to the decontamination area, before she runs out of food. However, shortly after Amanda reaches Ren, Amanda is kidnapped by Blanco and two other painballers. Toby finds Ren with a handful of other friends from the Gardeners who have also survived. The two narrative threads intersect when Toby and Ren then follow tracks in search of Amanda and arrive on the beach just as Snowman/Jimmy is approaching the new humans he'd discovered at the end of *Oryx and Crake*. These men have Amanda with them, though she's now weak from days of abuse and rape. This novel concludes that night, just hours after the end of *Oryx and Crake*, when Ren, Toby, Amanda and Jimmy sit around a campfire, with the painballers subdued and tied to a tree, as they are approached by flickering torches and singing in the moonlight: the Crakers, looking for their guardian Snowman/Jimmy, draw near.

MaddAddam (2013)

MaddAddam begins where the first two novels end, although much of the narrative is told through recounted stories that take place earlier still, particularly in the childhoods and adolescence of brothers Adam and Zeb. At the start of this novel, the guileless Crakers are conned by the painballers into undoing their ropes, and the men escape. The Gardeners, MaddAddamites (a more radical splinter group of Gardeners) and Crakers build a camp, and in it they grow vegetables, try to nurse Amanda and

Snowman/Jimmy back to health and search for missing friends while fending off the painballers who roam loose now.

Throughout the novel, Toby tells the Crakers stories, as Snowman used to, while Snowman/Jimmy is too sick to do so. One young Craker, Blackbeard, becomes devoted to Toby. He watches Toby keep a journal of events as they unfold, and she teaches Blackbeard to write. Humans and Crakers come to mate first through a terrible misunderstanding in which Amanda, after her ordeal during the abduction by painballers, and while still weak and sick, is gang raped by male Crakers who believe she is blue (fertile) and therefore willing. The lack of intent behind the Crakers' rape is important even to Amanda, who talks about giving away her baby or giving it to the pigoons to eat if it is human (and therefore the product of her brutal raping by the painballers). Thus, all are relieved when the first human-Craker hybrid is born. Swift Fox and Ren also give birth to hybrid children by the end of the trilogy. This is a human hybridisation with an alien/Other species that seems hopeful, and part of a future that's full of singing and stories, quite removed from the fear of miscegenation that populated much early science fiction. It seems likely that Crakers and hybrids will form future generations, should they survive long enough. The group of Gardeners, MaddAddamites and Crakers eventually defeat the painballers in a final battle by partnering with the pigoons, genetically modified animals created by former corporations, who we discover can talk with the Crakers. Much of the narrative is a recording of the oral stories as Toby explains events and the world to the Crakers. The novel ends with a final chapter in which Toby has gone but is remembered and recorded by the new author, Blackbeard.

Science Fiction and Ecofeminist Critiques of Big Business

While there are many threats to individual, group and global survival within Atwood's trilogy, the most systemic and pervasive is capitalism and its value system predicated upon individualism and profit. Like much science fiction, the *MaddAddam* novels reflect contemporary anxiety about growing corporate domination and are part of a recent tradition of science fiction in that vein. Indeed, science fiction critic Eric Otto has identified "unfettered capitalist development" (101) and "anxieties about capitalist production and consumption patterns" (100) in texts by authors including Robinson, Pohl, Kornbluth, Le Guin, Piercy, Callenbach and others. Science fiction scholar Lisa Yaszek has noted that scholars including Darko Suvin and Fredric Jameson sometimes even talk about science fiction as "THE literature of late capitalism" because it so effectively captures the experience of living in a high-tech world. (46)

Capitalist critiques feature in science fiction and utopian/dystopian writing, perhaps beginning with Sir Thomas More's early *Utopia* (1516) (in which More imagines a country with no private property, where men are free to enter each other's houses, and citizens rotate homes every ten years), and with contemporary examples abounding.[1] In contemporary dystopian visions in general, then, Big Brother has often been replaced by "Big Business". However, capitalism is a particular concern of women's science fiction writing because of the way in which women have historically been excluded and exploited by the capitalist market system.[2] Thus, Atwood continues in a tradition of feminist science fiction writers who have critiqued capitalism, including Charlotte Perkins Gilman with *Herland* (1915) and Ursula K. Le Guin in *The Dispossessed* (1974), for example. What Atwood adds to the body of feminist science fiction is an *ecofeminist* critique of capitalism and its implications for the environment and its inhabitants.

In two central philosophical ways, ecofeminism finds itself at odds with capitalism. First, capitalism in its current form works against ecofeminist goals at the material level by exploiting women and nature, both as resources and as labour (particularly the poor and non-white who traditionally have been tied most closely to nature). Second, capitalism relies upon a paradigm of thought that promotes individualism and instrumentalism, which are antithetical to the connections and relationships upon which ecofeminism is founded. Instrumentalism, in the ecofeminist context, is used to describe a world-view that dismisses any intrinsic significance and values something or someone only as a resource to another's end. Thus, ecofeminists use the term to describe an approach to

---

[1] Among many others, consider Neal Stephenson (*Snow Crash* 1992 and *The Diamond Age* 1995), Kim Stanley Robinson (for example his Mars Series—*Red Mars* 1993, *Green Mars* 1994, and *Blue Mars* 1996—in which he depicts corporations known as "Transnats" and later "Metanats" that become far more powerful than governments), Richard K. Morgan (most overtly *Market Forces* 2004) and Max Barry (who created privatised governments in *Jennifer Government* 2004 and *Machine Man* 2011).

[2] For a comprehensive analysis of gender-specific inequalities and exploitation under global capitalism see, for example, Maria Mies's "Dynamics of Sexual Division of Labor and Capital Accumulation" and Chandra Mohanty's comparative study of women workers in Silicon Valley, California, Narsapur, India, and Great Britain in *Feminism Without Borders*.

others that views women, nature and othered groups as resources and sees in them only use-value. Jytte Nhanenge, author of *Ecofeminism: Towards Integrating the Concerns of Women, Poor People, and Nature into Development,* identifies instrumentalism as part of a master-slave relationship within the system of dualisms that ecofeminism seeks to deconstruct. Nhanenge argues that the master-slave relationship is part of objectifying the Other, and she offers the following definition:

> *Instrumentalism* or *objectification:* The slave is obliged to put aside his or her own interests for the interests of the master. The slave is the master's instrument, a means to the master's ends. Hence, the master defines the slave's needs only in relation to his own needs. This objectifies the other. The slave is a resource for the master. Instrumental standards are judging the other into a good wife, an easy slave, a useful worker, etc. However, the slave is not a subject with intrinsic value. (113)

As a global patriarchal structure, capitalism, as ecofeminists, such as Carolyn Merchant and Karen Warren, complain, treats the world, including women and non-human nature, in just such a manner, seeing it only in terms of resources, interested only in their instrumental value. Ecofeminist Val Plumwood argues:

> The same basic structures of self which appear in the treatment of nature as lifeless instrument also underlie the rational egoism and instrumentalism of the market, the treatment of those supposedly less possessed of reason as inferior, and as instruments for their more civilized western neighbors (as in slavery, colonialism and racism), and the treatment of women as inferior others whose norms of virtue embody a thinly disguised instrumentalism. (143)

Thus, in contemplating a future of unfettered capitalism, the survival of women and nature, especially, is most imperilled.

Endangered World

There is a clear environmental warning in these novels. In the near-future world of the MaddAddam trilogy, humans, through industrialisation, capitalism and greed, have wrought destruction upon the natural world. The environment is a deteriorated and damaged one, as we quickly learn from the narrator in *Oryx and Crake*, who has to shield himself from the sun's dangerous rays and from rain that comes in such downpours it turns the air to mist (44). Jimmy's mother laments that her grandfather's grapefruit orchard "dried up like a giant raisin when the rains had stopped coming", their east-coast beach house disappeared under water, and the Everglades were on fire for three weeks (*Oryx and Crake* 63). In short, far-reaching climate change is underway by the time Jimmy is a child:

> The world has warmed […] the coastal aquifers turned salty and the northern permafrost melted […] the drought in the midcontinental plains region went on and on, and the Asian steppes turned to sand dunes, and meat became harder to come by. (*Oryx and Crake* 24)

Zeb, leader of the MaddAddamites, describes the "real action" of the corporations as "bulldozing the planet flat and grabbing anything of value" (*MaddAddam* 69).

In the society before the pandemic plague, known to the Gardeners as "the Flood", the government had mostly been replaced by corporations, which is likely why pollution and environmental destruction progressed to terrible degrees. For as Shiva, Mies, Plumwood and others argue, the capitalist approach relies upon instrumentalism and treating the world as a resource. Indeed, in *Ecofeminism Meets Business*, Chris Crittenden urges:

> In the age of corporate capitalism, where transnational corporations dwarf the power of many countries to resist their presence, expropriation of capital, and concomitant exploitation of natural resources, it becomes urgent to examine the beliefs that underlie the activities of business to determine if they are best for us and our planet. (51)

This is the lived reality of corporate capitalism from which Atwood extrapolates a future where business interests are the controlling ones. In her future world, some citizens reside in enclaves of different corporations.[3] The corporate enclaves, also referred to as "compounds", are surrounded by "Pleeblands" of disorder, corruption and filth. Those who are not employees of the major corporations or members of employees' families live in these dangerous and impoverished areas, without official identities, where there is pollution, scarcity, gangs and rampant crime. Even law and order are predominantly the purview of big business. The police enforce corporate regulations within the compounds and maintain compliance of citizen-workers; the force's name—CorpSeCorps—beautifully and sinisterly suggests the merging of death, "corpse", with (alleged) security, the "Sec"

---

[3] As we learn about the sex tourism industry in *Oryx and Crake*, we're told tourists go abroad to perform acts that "they'd be put in jail for back in their home countries" (89). This is one of the only references to the persistence of countries, but it's likely the jails and incarcerating authorities are corporate rather than state or national domain.

part of the name, the capitalist industries in the novel, frequently referred to as "the corps" (an abbreviation of corporations), and military units, "corps".

Agribusiness and Capitalist Abuse of Animals

Instrumentalism, as "the kind of use of an earth other which treats it as entirely a means to another's ends, as one whose being creates no limits on use and which can be entirely shaped to ends not its own" (Plumwood 142), is vividly demonstrated in these novels not only through the treatment of the environment, but also animals. Jimmy spends part of his childhood on OrganInc Farms because his father works on the "Pigoon Project". The "Farms" aspect is an ironic misnomer because, rather than resembling anything akin to a traditional farm, it is a highly industrialised and monitored compound. The project involves growing human-tissue organs in a transgenic host that can grow five or six kidneys at a time. As it is explained to Jimmy,

> Such a host animal could be reaped of its extra kidneys; then, rather than being destroyed, it could keep on living and grow more organs, much as a lobster could grow another claw to replace a missing one. That would be less wasteful, as it took a lot of food and care to grow a pigoon. A great deal of investment money had gone into OrganInc Farms. (*Oryx and Crake* 22-23)

While adopting such modifications is a sign of a progressive future in much science fiction, it is satirised by Atwood as a grotesque debasement of life. The pigoons are not contemplated as suffering animals or sentient beings, but only as sites of invested resources and potential returns. Ecofeminist and anti-globalisation activist Vandana Shiva describes cloning, genetic engineering and patenting of life as "the ultimate expression of the commercialization of science and the commodification of nature" (*Biopiracy* 24).

Atwood depicts the commercialisation and commodification of animals in horrific dystopian extremes, both through the medical industry, as with the Pigoon Project, and through meat production. The degradation of animals in the meat industry is best epitomised by the horrifying ChickieNobs. In an extreme extension of contemporary factory farming— or what anthropologist Barbara Noske has called the "the animal industrial complex"—headless chickens, full of antibiotics, are not raised as animals but produced as "meat-on-a-stick", with as few extraneous parts as possible.[4]

What animals become with the interference of corporate science, is, however, only part of the horror of the dystopia. The other equally horrifying part is what humans become as they control, use and abuse the animals and nature. Human indifference and desensitisation to animal suffering and debasement of non-human life is highlighted through Jimmy, who is initially distressed for the pigoons he sees at his father's work, and appalled by the "chicken" at NeoAgriculturals. Though he initially finds the chickens nightmarish and imagines that eating their deformed bodies would be akin to "eating a large wart" (*Oryx and Crake* 203), he becomes acclimatised and desensitised and is shown a few years later, in college, living almost exclusively off a diet of ChickieNobs and Buckets O'Nubbins.[5]

---

[4] The instrumental use of animals in this industry is well underway in reality, so that animals are contemplated not as whole creatures, but as useful parts; for example, parts of chickens—especially beaks—are already routinely removed, "trimmed", in the production of eggs, to avoid damage from pecking that would occur between birds caged together. However, unlike the headless chickens in *Oryx and Crake*, in the real world the majority of chickens intended for meat consumption are killed before six weeks of age, the stage at which beaks are trimmed (Hester and Shea-Moore). Increasingly, animals, plants and organisms are being altered to better suit their intended purpose as human food, medicine or research. Genetically modified organisms (GMOs) are becoming commonplace, particularly transgenic plants, which might be used for biopharmaceuticals and are commonly used for food; for example, many crops are being produced to be pest-resistant, and a California company (later acquired by Monsanto) created the Flavr-savr tomato, with delayed ripening to improve shelf-life and taste. The first genetically modified animal bred for food in the United States is the AquAdvantage salmon, which has been altered to grow year round and can reach consumable size in half the time of regular salmon (eighteen months rather than three years). Data on the AquAdvantage salmon was submitted to the FDA for approval in 1996, but approval of the fish—nicknamed "Frankenfish" by objectors—has been delayed by protests, further studies and public comment periods. The FDA has not yet issued its decision, but found "no significant impact" in its study of the fish and the extended public comment period ended in May 2013 (FDA). The fish was cleared for production of eggs in Canada in December 2013, though the sale of such eggs or the fish itself has not yet been approved (AquaBounty Technologies).

[5] Of course ChickieNobs are not dissimilar in name to chicken nuggets, and Buckets O'Nubbins is clearly intended to bring to mind contemporary fast-food chicken, since fried chicken is about the only food sold in "buckets". The cognitive disconnect between the knowledge of what goes into food and the choice to consume it anyway is satirised in these names, and Jimmy's diet of grotesque

The capitalist instrumentalism that abuses and denigrates animals and nature predictably also extends to humans, and especially women. The most pronounced commodification of human bodies is that of women's and children's bodies in the sex industry and child trafficking. Oryx is a primary example because she has been bought and sold from an early age: she is first sold to a man named "Uncle En", who wants her to market flowers to tourists in the city; after his murder, she becomes the property of a child pornographer, and later she becomes a sex worker in America, where she works off the cost of her entry to the country through pornography for a pimp in California. It is not clear how she escapes the California basement where she begins the U.S. chapter of her life, but her objectification and commodification has been institutionalised by the time Crake finds her through "student services" at the university he attends (Jimmy jokes that Oryx *was* the "service" [*Oryx and Crake* 310]).

Oryx herself is pragmatic and resigned to her interpolation into the capitalist system. She dispassionately explains to Jimmy the benefits of having a monetary value of the kind that has been clearly and repeatedly placed upon her:

> Of course (said Oryx), having a money value was no substitute for love. Every child should have love. Every person should have it. She herself would rather have had her mother's love [...] but love was undependable, it came and then it went, so it was good to have a money value, because then at least those who wanted to make a profit from you would make sure you were fed enough and not damaged too much. Also, there were many who had neither love nor a money value, and having one of these things was better than having nothing. (*Oryx and Crake* 126)

Thus, within a capitalist system, Oryx understands that having a monetary value is a way to survive.

In the future U.S., unwanted women are disposed of and even literally consumed. In Oryx's home country, they're thrown in rivers, but, in Jimmy's, the meat grinders of a fast-food chain help to clean up the streets of dead prostitutes and other victims of mob violence. In the production of SecretBurgers, women and animal flesh are literally indistinguishable:

> The secret of SecretBurgers was that no one knew what sort of animal

---

chicken pieces is clearly meant to invoke parallels to the real-life dissociation between animal and meat product by our contemporary fast-food industry, as well as the wide-spread lack of conscious, intellectual and emotional connection to food. It is not coincidental that Atwood adopted a vegetarian diet for her tour with the second book in this trilogy, *The Year of the Flood*.

protein was actually in them [...] The meat grinders weren't 100 per cent efficient; you might find a swatch of cat fur in your burger or a fragment of mouse tail. Was there a human fingernail, once?

It was possible. The local pleebmobs paid the CorpSeCorpsMen to turn a blind eye. In return, the CorpSeCorps let the pleebmobs run the low-level kidnappings and assassinations, [...] they also ran corpse disposals, harvesting organs for transplant, then running the gutted carcasses through the SecretBurgers grinders. So went the worst rumors. During the glory days of SecretBurgers, there were very few bodies found in vacant lots. (*The Year of the Flood* 33)

The furtive, involuntary cannibalism is reminiscent of the dystopian future of *Make Room! Make Room!*—Harry Harrison's 1966 novel that was made into the cult hit *Soylent Green*—but also of Atwood's own recurring metaphor of women devoured by society. In Atwood's very first novel, *The Edible Woman* (1969), the protagonist, Marian, after becoming engaged, finds herself unable to eat as she increasingly identifies and empathises with the food, beginning with meat but encompassing eggs and vegetables as the story progresses. That novel concludes with Marion's realisation that her fiancé is consuming her, and so she bakes a cake of a woman and offers him that instead. When he refuses, she eats the woman-cake herself.[6] In the *MaddAddam* trilogy, though, it is not a fiancé or individual, or even single institution (such as marriage) consuming women but more explicitly society at large. Most often their consumption here is concomitant to their association with animals so that the hierarchical view of nature and animals is extended to treat women's bodies as disposable and as mere resource.

Within the capitalist society of the *MaddAddam* series, women's bodies become commodities perhaps most explicitly through the booming sex industry. This is also where we can see women most closely linked to and depicted as animals. For example, the sex club where Ren works and then waits out the Flood is called Scales and Tails, and the performers there are bejewelled and fish- or bird-like. It's likely here that Crake takes Jimmy after Jimmy's mother has died, and Jimmy finds himself

being worked over by two girls covered from head to toe in sequins that were glued onto their skin and shimmered like the scales of a virtual fish. (*Oryx and Crake* 289)

---

[6] The topic of women's relationships to food recurs in many of Atwood's novels, including *Lady Oracle*, in which the protagonist, Joan, battles with her mother over control of her body and particularly its size. See Parker's "You Are What You Eat" (1995) for a broader discussion of the role of food in several of Atwood's novels.

In addition, the female performer, Katrina Wu, who captivates Zeb as he's travelling undercover before he joins the Gardeners, is a snake handler with snakeskin and bird outfits (171). In the following exchange with Toby, Zeb explains how men like to think of women as animals:

> "What is it about women and snakes?" says Toby. "Or women and birds, for that matter."
> "We like to think you're wild animals," says Zeb. "Underneath the decorations."
> "You mean stupid or subhuman?"
> "Cut me some slack here. I mean, ferociously out of control, in a good way. A scaly, feathery woman is a powerful attraction. She's got an edge to her, like a goddess. Risky. Extreme." (*MaddAddam* 171-2)

Thus it seems the connection between women and animals in this society is used to exoticise, eroticise, Other and objectify. In a society that exploits animals and destroys the natural environment, the association with them is a dangerous one.

Men do not escape the capitalist abuses; they are part of the system, too, though usually better positioned within it—where Oryx is sold as a child, Jimmy is "bid on" by universities when he finishes school. The animalisation of specific men is part of their positioning as objects for (ab)use and sexualisation, just as it is for women. For example, the painballers are criminals who have been incarcerated and made to fight to the death to survive in an arena. This battle is televised for public entertainment and profit, and reminiscent of cock-fighting or dog-fighting. Those who survive are feared because the violence they've endured and exerted has made them brutal, but they also are treated, like the animalised women, as sources of eroticism and as exotic curios; thus they are given invitations to dinner parties of corporate execs, and even paid for sex by some of the elite wives.

Just as women have been exoticised in part through their association with animals, there seems to have been an exponential rise in animal fetishes and bestiality. In fact, animal fetishes are so prevalent that when Toby takes a job as a "furzooter", carrying an advertising sign, dressed as an animal with a cartoon head, she's routinely sexually attacked:

> In the first week she suffered three attacks by fetishists who knocked her over, twisted the big head around so she was blinded, and rubbed their pelvises against her fur, making strange noises, of which the meows were most recognizable. It wasn't rape—no part of her actual body was touched—but it was creepy. (*The Year of the Flood* 31)

Crakers: Ecological Solution

In light of the exploitation and the abuse of the earth, animals and other humans, then, the desire of the misanthropic, brilliant scientist Crake to wipe out the human species and begin again with something he designed to be better is somewhat understandable. Jayne Glover, in her article "Human/Nature: Ecological Philosophy in Margaret Atwood's *Oryx and Crake*", suggests that, given this context, Crake strives for a "pre-lapsarian world" (55). Human activity in the novel is precipitating environmental catastrophes, such as global warming, and the natural world has been reduced to "instrument or object" (Glover 52), or, in more ecofeminist terms, the instrumentalist paradigm. To achieve a more harmonious relationship between people and nature, Crake needs to redesign not only society, as in much utopian fiction, but also humans to create a less aggressive and more ecological people. The Crakers offer an alternative to the violence of capitalism and patriarchy, through practices that connect them to nature. Atwood reveals:

> One of the questions the novel grapples with is: how would human beings have to be altered so that they would avoid the major problems that bedevil us today? Thus were born the Crakers—bio-engineered to have built-in sunblock and insect repellent, equipped with self-healing purring capabilities, and designed to be seasonal maters so they will never suffer from sexual jealousy. No agriculture is needed by them, as they are totally vegetarian and can eat leaves; no money is required, as there is nothing they have to buy or exchange; they will wage no wars, as they have no need for territory that they have to acquire or defend from invasion. ("Margaret Atwood's Trilogy")

Thus, the lack of property and capitalism, along with the built-in bug-spray, is part of the solution.

In addition to remodelling people, Atwood revises dominant narratives about animals and humans' hierarchical relationship to them. In this trilogy, even the animals created by human society—such as the engineered wolvogs, rakunks and pigoons—despite being designed to serve human interests, are revealed to have their own communities and cultures as the narrative progresses. Most clearly we see this with the pigoons, who have developed their own language, something often pointed to as a marker of culture. In fact, we learn that the pigoons have a language not only internally but one that the Crakers can understand. Thus the humans have to rework the Creation Story for the Crakers to recognise that they are not the only animals with culture and language:

> And Crake thought that you had eaten all the words, so there were none
> left over for the animals, and that was why they could not speak. But he
> was wrong about that. Crake was not always right about everything.
>
> Because when he was not looking, some of the words fell out of the
> egg onto the ground, and some fell into the water, and some blew away in
> the air. And none of the people saw them. But the animals and the birds
> and the fish did see them, and ate them up. They were a different kind of
> word, so it was sometimes hard for people to understand the animals. They
> had chewed the words up too small.
>
> And the Pigoons—the Pig Ones—ate up more of the words than any of
> the other animals did. You know how they love to eat. So the Pig Ones can
> think very well. (*MaddAddam* 290)

In *MaddAddam,* the narrative suggests that the pigoons are the most
intelligent creatures, with superior mental faculties to the *un*modified
humans and wiser than the more naïve and unworldly Crakers.

When Jimmy asks Crake what the Crakers are being taught in the
Paradice Dome, Crake replies botany and zoology, what he summarises as
"what not to eat and what could bite. And what not to hurt" (309). I
believe this instruction "not to hurt" points to a different way of treating
others (including those of other species) that will not repeat the violence of
the past. It is also a crucial element in the development of the new people
as what ecofeminists like Plumwood and ecological philosophers like Arne
Næss call "ecological selves", beings who expand moral concern and care
beyond themselves or their own species.

The Crakers have been designed to be less aggressive than humans,
and they seem disinclined to fight or harm others; however, while they
may be predisposed towards ecological selfhood, this quality is not
entirely innate. For example, the biological safeguards to avoid sexual
competition suggest that Crake at least feared, in the wrong circumstances,
the Crakers could find conflict and perhaps become violent. If the quality
is at all innate, the repeated comparisons of the Crakers to children might
suggest that it's a possible trait for humans, too, at least those raised within
a different society—one without instrumentalist and exploitative
paradigms. The Crakers were bred for peacefulness and caring, as well as
taught it, and were sheltered from the violence of the previous society in
Paradice. Thus their innocence, genes and education separate them from
other populations such as the human and Pigoon survivors, who can
manifest caring, but can also vote for a death penalty for the painballers
(*MaddAddam* 369-370). In fact, when the prisoners have to be killed, the
Crakers are deliberately left behind while numerous humans and the band
of pigoons go down to the shore with a gun. The Craker Blackbeard
explains, "we did not go, we children of Crake, because Toby said it

would be hurtful to us" (*MaddAddam* 370). It's not certain whether it would be "hurtful" to the Crakers because it would upset them, given their nature, or damaging to their preserved innocence.

The teachings the Crakers receive, in Paradice, of "what not to hurt", in fact, encompass the natural world around them, and ensure they are not the destructive and exploitative creatures humans, on the whole, were. We see their care for nature on multiple occasions, as well as their spiritual connections to other creatures: for example, they utter blessings and prayers for forgiveness over the dead fish they are obliged to bring Snowman once a week and they also avoid eating animals themselves. In both of these actions, they mirror the existing practices of more ecologically-minded humans, particularly the group of vegetarian God's Gardeners. For some, vegetarianism or contextual vegetarianism (eating meat only under necessary circumstances and in the absence of alternative food sources) is an essential part of ecofeminism, and, as Greta Gaard notes,

> to date vegetarian ecofeminism has been explicitly articulated through the works of scholars and activists such as Carol Adams, Norma Benney, Lynda Birke, Deane Curtin, Josephine Donovan, Greta Gaard, Lori Gruen, Ronnie Zoe Hawkins, Marti Kheel, Brian Luke, Jim Mason, and Deborah Slicer. (118)

Vegetarianism is also a practice of eating lower on the food chain that can be advocated from an environmental perspective, as it was in Francis Lappé Moore's 1965 treatise *Diet for a Small Planet*. Thus, the Crakers demonstrate an ecofeminist alternative to the grotesque meat industry that was one of the most disturbing, instrumentalist degradations of life in the society that came before.

A New Kind of Last Man

Those who survive in these narratives are connected beings, part of caring communities, or, in ecofeminist terms, "selves in relation".[7] Even more radically, we come to understand that individual survival is not the point. We see perhaps the most striking development of a "Self-in-

---

[7] The "Self-in-Relation" and Plumwood's "Ecological Self" are developed from the vision of "Ecological Self" outlined by Arne Næss, founder of Deep Ecology. However, while indebted to the similar rejection of the individual self, ecofeminists have challenged some of the gendered assumptions about Deep Ecology's "Ecological Self". For a detailed analysis of this relationship between Deep Ecology and Ecofeminism, see Kheel, Spretnak and Zimmerman.

Relation" through Snowman's development from an initially immature and selfish character. Snowman serves as a kind of reluctant yet caring overseer of the Crakers. Dejected, lonely and frequently depressed, he is grumpy (sometimes telling them to leave him alone) but nevertheless benevolent. For example, when they turn up artefacts from life before the plague, Snowman lets them know whether they are dangerous or safe, warning them about "booby traps from the past". We also glimpse through the retrospectives a youth much like the rest of the uncaring society: he consumed ChickieNobs, hired prostitutes, one of which he remembers as "some tart he once bought" (*Oryx and Crake* 11), he consumed violence and porn online as entertainment, and even as a teen was interpolated into his father's sexist jokes and views of women, and he discarded girlfriends, including one of the other narrators, Ren, in high school. Jimmy as a teenager even consumed child pornography that fed the demand for human trafficking, child abuse and exploitation. Yet, in his haplessness, he fails to realise his own complicity and is able to direct his anger towards men who bought, sold and used Oryx in the past, while never contemplating his own role, even though he believes she's the very girl he watched online. Similarly, he played his part in bringing about the pandemic plague, for he wrote the advertising for the pill that spread it, and, while he didn't know about the plague, he was willing to promote a drug that would, he believed, sterilise people without their knowledge. Yet Jimmy is an affable protagonist in *Oryx and Crake* because despite his many faults he is not unkind; rather, he's a product of his terrible society, in which he seems somewhat lost and, by comparison to the canny and brilliant Glenn (Crake), appears quite artless. Despite a lack of deliberate malice, Jimmy is compliant in systems of exploitation and destruction because he fails or refuses to see the connections between patterns of consumption and exploitation, hierarchical thinking and lived exploitation. That he is a relatable and very average character serves as an indictment of our own society where most are not malevolent but can nonetheless be wilfully ignorant of the human and environmental exploitation that go into the capitalist production of goods they create demand for. Thus he is a very human (in every sense) protagonist who cares for the new species.

Although Jimmy is initially a begrudging caretaker, perhaps reluctantly fulfilling what seemed at the time a hypothetical promise to Oryx, and one with a beleaguered past of disinterest and complicity, he becomes a "Self-in-Relation" as he comes to care more for the Crakers than his own wellbeing and offers care without hope to benefit from it, beyond a fish a week. The protagonist of *Oryx and Crake* comes to cast off his self-absorption and the toxic influences of the capitalist society and to instead embrace caring relationships and community. By the time of *MaddAddam* he's willing to sacrifice his own survival for that of his community— which includes humans, Crakers and pigoons.

In fact, Snowman poses a possibility for a new ecofeminist iteration on a traditionally individualistic science fiction trope: the "Last Man" protagonist. Beginning with Mary Shelley's *The Last Man* in 1826, numerous apocalyptic science fiction stories have been told from the perspective of the "Last Man", including, perhaps most popularly, Richard Matheson's 1954 novel *I Am Legend*, which has seen a series of film adaptations (in 1964 as *The Last Man on Earth*, in 1971 as *The Omega Man* and in 2007 under its original title as *I Am Legend*). Many more involve a small band of survivors (the father/son duo in Cormac McCarthy's *The Road* and the small Californian community struggling for survival in Kim Stanley Robinson's *The Wild Shore: Three Californias*, for example). Earl G. Ingersoll, in his analysis of *Oryx and Crake,* also suggests Snowman "may be the most recent in a long line of fictional characters representing The Last Man", and "draws on the recent obsession in popular culture with The Survivor" (163). However, though Snowman is initially painted as possibly the lone human survivor after a pandemic plague, he is not alone. Where Last Man fiction previously focused on the survival of humans (beyond the isolated friendships of particular and usually domesticated animals, for example the dog in *I Am Legend*), Snowman's battle for survival extends to his young, genetically modified charges, whose survival he becomes more invested in than his own. At the end of *Oryx and Crake*, when he discovers there have been other men on the beach with guns, his mind races and he's unable to sleep, as he fears for the safety of the Crakers (365-66). He determines he will go to meet the armed strangers in an attempt at "presenting the Crakers to them in the proper light" (366). At the end of *Oryx and Crake*, he is weighing up the decision to join these men and abandon the Crakers or kill them to protect the innocent new race. As he contemplates joining the other humans, he worries about how best to prepare the Crakers to survive in his absence—whether he can give them something comforting to remember, instruct them to take noisy sticks (guns) and throw them into the ocean, or warn them about rape and slavery, concepts they won't understand (366-67). At the end of the second novel, *The Year of the Flood,* when Toby and Ren come across the painballers who have kidnapped Amanda, it seems Snowman must have resolved to kill the men to protect the Crakers: "He's carrying a spraygun, and he has it aimed at the two men. He's going to shoot them. He has that kind of maniac focus" (418). By the time of the final novel, *MaddAddam,* Snowman's willing to die so his community—which includes the Crakers—can survive. Thus, Snowman is the ultimate ecological Self-in-Relation because his community—unlike the traditional Last Man—has expanded to the non- and part-human characters and world around him.

Perhaps Snowman, and even the reader, should not necessarily hope for the survival of the human race, outside of the new Craker adaptation. It is poignant that the very lonely Snowman we meet on the beach at the start of the trilogy, daydreaming of human conversation, when he learns of other humans, rather than being excited, is full of fear for the Crakers. It speaks both to his compassion for the new people and his assessment of the quality of fellow human beings from the society before. Also, from an ecological view, eliminating the human population, along with their violent ways of interacting with the world, is not a tragedy, and can only be dystopian from an anthropocentric perspective. That is to say, given the depiction of human society before the "plague" or "Flood", and its catastrophic impact upon the rest of the natural world, for non-human nature, the wiping out of human neighbours is likely their best hope for survival.

Conclusion: Communal Survival through Ecofeminist Connections

Atwood's trilogy depicts a brutal and uncaring capitalist society that has devastated humans and non-humans alike. In the examples of the surviving Gardeners, MaddAddamites and Crakers, however, we are shown the possibility of practices of care that fundamentally undermine the hyper-individualism of the capitalist world before. The final narrator for the last chapter of the trilogy, at the close of *MaddAddam*, is the Craker Blackbeard, recoding a testimony of Toby's life. With the death of the former narrators, and most poignantly the Crakers' guardians, Snowman and Toby, the continuation of the story they are only one part of through these new people underscores that the survival that's important isn't individual or even necessarily human.

Works Cited

Atwood, Margaret. *The Edible Woman.* 1969. Reprint. New York: Bantman Books, 1991. Print.

—. *MaddAddam: A Novel.* New York: Nan A. Talese/Doubleday, 2013. Print.

—. "Margaret Atwood's trilogy draws on her visits to Australia, a disconcerting place". *The Australian,* August 31, 2013. Web. 22 October 2013.

—. *Oryx and Crake: A Novel.* New York: Nan A. Talese/Doubleday, 2003. Print.

—. *Surfacing.* New York: Simon and Schuster, 1972. Print.

—. *Survival: A Thematic Guide to Canadian Literature.* 1972. Reprint. Ontario: McClelland & Stewart, 2004. Print.

—. *The Year of the Flood: A Novel.* New York: Nan A. Talese/Doubleday, 2009. Print.

Barry, Max. *Jennifer Government: A Novel.* New York: Doubleday, 2003. Print.

—. *Machine Man.* New York: Vintage Contemporaries, 2011. Print.

Crittenden, Chris. "Ecofeminism Meets Business: a Comparison of Ecofeminist, Corporate, and Free Market Ideologies". *Journal of Business Ethics* 24.1 (2000): 51-63. Print.

Dillon, Grace L. "Indigenous Scientific Literacies in Nalo Hopkinson's Ceremonial Worlds". *Journal of the Fantastic in the Arts* 18.1 (2007): 23-41. Print.

—. *Walking the Clouds: An Anthology of Indigenous Science Fiction.* Tucson: University of Arizona Press, 2012. Print.

Gaard, Greta C. "Vegetarian Ecofeminism: a Review Essay". *Frontiers: a Journal of Women Studies* 23.3 (2002): 117-146. Print.

Gibson, William. *Neuromancer.* New York: Ace Books, 1984. Print.

Gilman, Charlotte P. *Herland.* 1915. Reprint. New York: Pantheon, University of Virginia Library, 1979. Print.

Glover, Jayne. "Human/Nature: Ecological Philosophy in Margaret Atwood's *Oryx and Crake*". *English Studies in Africa* 52.2 (2009): 50-62. Print.

Harrison, Harry. *Make Room! Make Room!* 1966. Reprint. New York: Orb Books, 2008. Print.

Hester, P. Y. and M. Shea-Moore. "Reviews—Beak Trimming Egg-Laying Strains of Chickens". *World's Poultry Science Journal* 59.4 (2003): 458. Print.

Howells, Coral Ann. "Margaret Atwood's Dystopian Visions: *The Handmaid's Tale* and *Oryx and Crake*". *The Cambridge Companion to Margaret Atwood.* Ed. Coral Ann Howells. Cambridge: Cambridge University Press, 2006. 161-175. Print.

I Am Legend. Dir. Francis Lawrence. Burbank, CA: Warner Home Video, 2007. Film.

Ingersoll, Earl G. "Survival in Margaret Atwood's Novel *Oryx and Crake*". *Extrapolation* 45.2 (2004): 162-175. Print.

Kheel, Marti. "Ecofeminism and Deep Ecology: Reflections on Identity and Difference". *Covenant for a New Creation: Ethics, Religion, and Public Policy*. Eds. Carol S. Robb and Carl J. Casebolt. New York: Orbis Books, 1991. 142-45. Print.

Lappé, Francis Moore. *Diet for a Small Planet*. 1965. Reprint. New York: Ballentine Books, Random House, 1971. Print.

Le Guin, U. K. *The Dispossessed: An Ambiguous Utopia*. New York: Harper & Row, 1974. Print.

Matheson, Richard. *I Am Legend*. 1954. Reprint. New York: Walker, 1970. Print.

McCarthy, Cormac. *The Road*. New York: Alfred A. Knopf, 2006. Print.

Merchant, Carolyn. *Radical Ecology*. New York: Routledge, 1992. Print.

—. *The Death of Nature: Women, Ecology and the Scientific Revolution*. San Francisco: Harper and Row, 1980. Print.

Mies, Maria. "Dynamics of Sexual Division of Labour and Capital Accumulation: Women Lace Workers of Narsapur". *Economic and Political Weekly* 16.10 (1981): 487-500. Print.

—, and Vandana Shiva. *Ecofeminism*. New York: Palgrave, 1993. Print.

—. *Patriarchy and Accumulation on a World Scale: Women and the International Division of Labour*. London: Zed Books, 1986. Print.

Mohanty, Chandra Talpade. *Feminism without Borders: Decolonizing Theory, Practicing Solidarity*. Durham & London: Duke University Press, 2003. Print.

More, Thomas. *Utopia*. 1516. Reprint. Amsterdam: Theatrum Orbis Terrarum, 1969. Print.

Morgan, Richard K. *Market Forces*. New York: Del Rey/Ballentine Books, 2005. Print.

Næss, Arne. "The shallow and the deep, long-range ecology movement. A summary". *Inquiry* 16:1 (1973): 95-100. Print.

Nhanenge, Jytte. *Ecofeminism: Towards Integrating the Concerns of Women, Poor People, and Nature into Development*. Lanham, Md: University Press of America, 2011. Print.

Noske, Barbara. *Beyond Boundaries: Humans and Other Animals*. Montreal: Black Rose Books, 1989. Print.

Otto, Eric C. *Green Speculations: Science Fiction and Transformative Environmentalism*. Columbus: Ohio State University Press, 2012. Print.

Parker, Emma. "You are What You Eat: The Politics of Eating in the Novels of Margaret Atwood". *Twentieth Century Literature* 41.3 (1995): 349-368. Print.

Plumwood, Val. *Feminism and the Mastery of Nature*. London: Routledge, 1993. Print.

Robinson, Kim S. *Blue Mars*. New York: Bantam Books, 1996. Print.

—. *Green Mars*. New York: Bantam Books, 1994. Print.

—. *Red Mars*. New York: Bantam Books, 1993. Print.

—. *The Wild Shore*. New York: Berkley Pub. Group, 1984. Print.

Shelley, Mary Wollstonecraft and Hugh J. Luke. *The Last Man*. Lincoln: University of Nebraska Press, 1965. Print.

Shiva, Vandana. *Biopiracy: The Plunder of Nature and Knowledge*. Boston, Massachusetts: South End Press, 1997. Print.

—. *Stolen Harvest: The Hijacking of the Global Food Supply*. Cambridge, Massachusetts: South End Press, 2000. Print.

Soylent Green. Dir. Richard Fleischer. Metro-Goldwyn-Mayer, 1973. Theatrical.

Spretnak, Charlene. "Radical Nonduality in Ecofeminist Philosophy". *Ecofeminism: Women, Culture, Nature*. Ed. Karen J. Warren. Bloomington: Indiana University Press, 1997. 425-436. Print.

Squier, Susan. "A Tale Meant to Inform, Not to Amuse: *Oryx and Crake*. A Novel". *Science* 302.5648 (2003): 1154-1155. Print.

Stephenson, Neal. *Snow Crash*. New York: Bantam Books, 1992. Print.

—. *The Diamond Age*. New York: Bantam Books, 2003. Print.

Suvin, Darko. *Metamorphoses of Science Fiction: On the Poetics and History of a Literary Genre*. New Haven: Yale University Press, 1979. Print.

The Last Man on Earth. Dir. Ubaldo Ragona, American International Pictures, 1964. Theatrical.

The Omega Man. Dir. Boris Sagal. Walter Seltzer Productions, 1971. Theatrical.

Warren, Karen J., ed. *Ecofeminism: Women, Culture, Nature*. Bloomington and Indianapolis: Indiana University Press, 1997. Print.

—. *Ecofeminist Philosophy: A Western Perspective on What it is and Why It Matters*. Lanham: Rowman & Littlefield Publishers, 2000. Print.

—. "The Power and the Promise of Ecological Feminism". *Environmental Ethics* 12.2 (1990): 125-46. Print.

—. "Toward an Ecofeminist Ethic". *Studies in the Humanities* 15.2 (1988): 140-56. Print.

Yaszek, Lisa. "Afrofuturism, Science Fiction, and the History of the Future". *Socialism and Democracy* 20.3 (2006): 41-60. Print.

Zimmermann, Michael E. "Deep Ecology and Ecofeminism: The Emerging Dialogue". *Reweaving the World*. Ed. Irene Diamond and Gloria Orenstein. San Francisco: Sierra Club Books, 1990. 138-154. Print.

CONTRIBUTORS

Anna Bedford earned her Ph.D. in Comparative Literature from the University of Maryland, College Park, with a dissertation focused on Canadian science fiction. While a student at Maryland, she also completed a Graduate Certificate in Women's Studies and won the University of Maryland's Graduate Student Distinguished Service Award. She holds an M.A. (honours) from the University of Edinburgh, Scotland, where she did her undergraduate work in English Literature. Anna has had several articles on women's SF accepted for publication and is currently engaged in a book project anthologising early women SF writers of the pulp and magazine era. She teaches English at the University of Maryland, and lives in a cooperative community in Greenbelt, Maryland—a place of utopian aspirations—with her husband, Barrett, their son, Callum, and Golden Retriever, Dougal.

Anna Lindhé is a postdoctoral fellow at the Department of Culture and Media Studies at Umeå University, Sweden. She has a Ph.D. in English Literature from Lund University. Her dissertation, *Appropriations of Shakespeare's* King Lear *in Three Modern North American Novels*, won the Margaret Atwood Society Award for best dissertation on Atwood. A chapter from her dissertation ("Sisterhood, Shame, and Redemption in *Cat's Eye* and *King Lear*") appeared in *Margaret Atwood Studies*, Vol 7, 2013. She is currently working on a project called "Literature and the Paradox of Narrative Empathy". She has also published on George Eliot and empathy in the Swedish language.

Meredith Minister is an Assistant Professor of Religion at Shenandoah University in Winchester, VA where she teaches Food and Religion, Gender and Religion, and History of Western Christianity. She completed graduate degrees at Southern Methodist University and Boston University and has served as Department Chair and Assistant Professor of Religion at Kentucky Wesleyan College. Her publications include *Trinitarian Theology and Power Relations: God Embodied* as well as articles in the *Journal of Feminist Studies in Religion* and *Disability Studies Quarterly*.

Lauren Rule Maxwell is an Associate Professor of English at The Citadel in Charleston, South Carolina. A native of Richmond, Virginia, she graduated from Wake Forest University with a B.A. in English and a minor in Biology. After writing professionally for healthcare organisations in Washington, D.C., she earned her M.A. and Ph.D. from Emory University. She teaches courses on American literature, Caribbean literature, professional writing and composition, and she participates in the Lowcountry Writing Project, Charleston's site for the National Writing Project. Her monograph, *Romantic Revisions in Novels of the Americas*, was published in 2013 by Purdue University Press. She has written about Margaret Atwood's fiction in *Modern Fiction Studies* and *Margaret Atwood Studies*, about F. Scott Fitzgerald's *The Great Gatsby* in *The F. Scott Fitzgerald Review* and about consumer culture and advertising in the recent Cambridge University Press volume *F. Scott Fitzgerald in Context*.

Patricia A. Stapleton is a comparative political science and public policy scholar. She currently teaches at Worcester Polytechnic Institute in Massachusetts, where she is also the Director of the Society, Technology and Policy Program. Her research interests cover the regulation of biotechnology, both in food production and reproductive medicine. In addition to a Ph.D. in Political Science, Patricia also has a Masters in French Literature. When possible, she writes on the intersection of literature and politics, especially in the context of dystopian fiction.

Karma Waltonen asked people to join her for a weekly meeting of The Margaret Atwood Book Club in 2005, to help with her dissertation: *Reading Margaret Atwood in Theory and Practice: Active Reading, Witnessing, and Community*. When the project was done, they wanted to keep coming, to keep reading, although they have had to read some non-Atwood now and again. Waltonen is the former President of the Margaret Atwood Society and is the current editor of *Margaret Atwood Studies*. She teaches a variety of writing courses in the University Writing Program at The University of California—Davis, in addition to courses on graphic novels, science & literature, writing and performing stand-up comedy, and *The Simpsons*. She co-authored *The Simpsons in the Classroom: Embiggening the Learning Experience with the Wisdom of Springfield* in 2010. Recent publications include articles on time travel in *Star Trek*, the ethics of religious cults in *Doctor Who*, and, of course, Margaret Atwood.

Miles Weafer is a doctoral candidate in the Joint Graduate Program in Communication & Culture at York University in Toronto. Drawing on policy deliberations, public meetings and online forums surrounding the Canadian Broadcasting Corporation (CBC)'s 2012 license renewal hearings, Miles' dissertation addresses the perceived role and scope of Canada's national public broadcaster amidst CBC's extension online. While his current work in Canadian Communication Studies focuses on the history and development of public broadcasting in Canada, Miles has a background in Cultural Studies and English (M.A., McMaster University, 2009; B.A., Trent University, 2005), and a long-standing interest in Canadian literature and the mythology of Canadian nationalism. Miles' interest in "Speculative Fiction" derives from his undergraduate years in English and Cultural Studies at Trent University in Peterborough, Ontario, Canada.